Enigma Variations

ENIGMA VARIATIONS

LOVE, WAR & BLETCHLEY PARK

Irene Young

MAINSTREAM
PUBLISHING

EDINBURGH AND LONDON

First published in Great Britain in 1990 by
MAINSTREAM PUBLISHING COMPANY (EDINBURGH) LTD
7 Albany Street
Edinburgh EH1 3UG

ISBN 1 84018 377 2

This edition, 2000

A catalogue record for this book is available from the British Library

Typeset in Typewriter and Van Dijck
Printed and bound in Great Britain by Cox and Wyman Ltd

To the Memory of the Four Cousins

To skies that knit their heartstrings right,
To fields that bred them brave,
The saviours come not home to-night:
Themselves they could not save.

A.E.H.

ACKNOWLEDGEMENTS

I wish to thank the following people for their kind permission for use of material: Marjorie Lingen-Hutton ('Tam i' th' Kirk' by Violet Jacob, from *Scottish Love Poems*, edited by Antonia Fraser); *Encounter* ('Wolverton' passage by John Vaizey); HMSO (*The Tiger Kills: The Story of the Indian Division in the North African Campaign*, published for the Government of India); Allen Lane (Viking) (*The Hut Six Story* by Gordon Welchman); Peter Calvocoressi (*Top Secret Ultra* by Peter Calvocoressi); Thorsons Publishers Ltd ('Bletchley Park' verses from *Women In Air Force Blue* by Beryl Escott).

For assistance and information of various kinds I am indebted to the Rt. Hon. Roy Bradford, PC; Mr Tony Geraghty; the Very Revd Dr J. Fraser McLuskey, MC; Air Commodore H.A. Probert, MBE, RAF (Retd) of the Ministry of Defence; Mr Trevor Royle; Lieut-Col (QM) I.F. Smith, MBE, Secretary of the SAS Regimental Association; and Major John Wiseman, MC.

Debts of a more personal nature I owe to Mrs L.E. Colledge; Dr Gilbert Kennedy; Dr Donald MacLean; Mrs F.C. Matheson; Dr and Mrs Murray Simpson; and the Revd R.W. Smith.

My deepest gratitude must be reserved for my son, Dr Iain Gordon Brown, who read my manuscript, checked military details, and gave me advice throughout. Most of all I thank him for his never-failing encouragement, and his boundless enthusiasm for a project which, for obvious reasons, he need not have made his own, but which he did, unstintingly, for my sake.

INTRODUCTION

In my life during the Second World War there were three enigmas.

Central in time was the one officially so named: the German *Enigma* encyphering machine, the decoded signals from which were referred to by British Intelligence as the Ultra Secret – or 'Ultra'. I worked in the Foreign Office, in Government Communications Headquarters (formerly the Government Code & Cypher School) at Bletchley Park.

In his book *Most Secret War* Professor R.V. Jones calls Ultra 'the greatest intelligence triumph of all time'; and Ralph Bennett, author of *Ultra in the West*, describes 'the feat of cryptography, mathematics and electrical engineering which made the decoding possible' as 'marvels without parallel'. The ability to decode the Wehrmacht's wireless communications gave the Allies the opportunity to 'see into the enemy's mind'.

It was only in 1977 that the official ban on any reference to Ultra was lifted, although three years before this date Group Captain F.W. Winterbotham had been the first to break the silence with *The Ultra Secret*. This pioneering book was written without access to official documents. The deposit of Ultra material in the Public Records Office in 1977 was the signal for a number of authors to produce a series of important works. *Ultra Goes to War: the Secret Story* by Ronald Lewin appeared in 1978. This was followed by Jozef Garlinski's *Intercept: the*

Enigma War (1979); Peter Calvocoressi's *Top Secret Ultra* (1980); and *The Hut Six Story: Breaking the Enigma Code* by Gordon Welchman, which was published in 1982. Peter Calvocoressi had already made three excellent radio broadcasts, and the scripts were published in *The Listener* in 1977.

All these books and talks dealt mainly with the technicalities and amazing complexity of the Enigma machine – the vehicle for the principal cypher of the German armed forces – and with the breaking of the code and the interpretation of the intelligence decrypts. Christopher Andrew's *Secret Service* (1985) sets the world of the Bletchley Park cryptanalysts, their masters and their minions, within the whole fabric of a developing British 'intelligence community'. Nigel West, in *GCHQ: the Secret Wireless War 1900–86* (1986) establishes the work we did at Bletchley in historical and current context. Revelation of the crucial importance of Ultra and of the achievement of GCHQ at Bletchley – GC & CS as it was still sometimes called – has afforded a new perspective on the conduct of the war. The four magisterial volumes of F.H. Hinsley's *British Intelligence in the Second World War: Its Influence on Strategy and Operations* (1979–88) chronicle in great detail the cryptanalytic successes and the effect the intelligence they produced had on the outcome of events on land, sea and in the air. Ralph Bennett's study *Ultra in the West* (1979) sets out the history of the Normandy campaign in terms of the intelligence produced by Ultra.

However, as Max Hastings observed in his foreword to the 1988 reissue of Lewin's *Ultra Goes to War*, much of the official writing about the work at Bletchley Park has been criticised for its dullness. Sir Maurice Oldfield, the distinguished head of the Secret Intelligence Service in the 1970s, is said to have dismissed Hinsley's and his collaborators' exhaustive studies (which, as Hastings remarks, carefully eschew personalities) as 'history without people'. The humanity that was Bletchley has been overwhelmed by the adulation of its corporate genius. To my knowledge, there has been nothing about the daily circumstances of life for those who worked at Bletchley Park, save only a short chapter in Gordon Welchman's *The Hut Six Story* and passing references in Calvocoressi's book; and these passages treat of the life of the brilliant code-breakers and cryptanalysts, who lived a donnish domestic existence in pubs and country cottages. Those of us – young service personnel and temporary civil servants, who were the cogs in the great enterprise – *we* have not had our story told. Peculiar to us were the real discomforts and the grim humour of life in forced billets. My book has, therefore, a totally different and much humbler purpose than those cited above. It gives, perhaps, a 'worm's eye' view of Bletchley, to complement the reminiscences of the more elevated denizens of this remarkable establishment. This is one woman's account of her experiences and of the social conditions at 'BP' – Enigma variations of a particular kind.

Ours in the rank and file was not the individual genius of the code-breakers. We, the 'highly sophisticated rank and file', as Gordon Welchman was pleased to call us, were the adjutants: but nonetheless, collectively, what we did was crucial. If we were linguists, our task was translation; otherwise, it was operating the decoding machines, or recording, plotting and tabulating – work that was essential and meticulous, but repetitive and wearying. That we had to be mentally acute went without saying, but the greatest requirement was integrity: the ability to guard, against all temptation, the secret of this most vital source of intelligence.

In talking of that cardinal rule of security in the shadowy world of intelligence designated 'the need to know', one of Bletchley's brilliant mathematicians explained that 'people who were not at the top did not know much about matters that were not directly of their concern'. Equally it can be said that those at the top did not altogether perceive the circumstances of those at the lower end of the BP ladder; for conditions varied from dreary billets and night bus journeys across two counties, to private car transport and chintzy domesticity.

It is true that the clever young men at Bletchley Park did work of paramount importance, but I often felt that they did not fully appreciate just how their cleverness insulated them from the dangerous and brutish aspects of the war. As Ralph Bennett admitted, 'Security regulations and shift-working combined to create an inward-looking habit of mind. He went on to declare that, 'Bletchley wives with young children had a miserable war: not permitted to know until 30 years later what it was that took their husbands away at all hours of the day and night with the rotation of shift-work and returned them tired, uncommunicative and irritable, they bore their lot as cheerfully as they could.'

ENIGMA VARIATIONS

As a wife at Bletchley, though not a Bletchley wife, I would willingly have suffered those inconveniences.

★ ★ ★

Above all, this is my personal testament, an account of developing character from the year before Munich to the year after the war, where are revealed further variations on the Enigma theme. I was not permitted even to mention let alone to write about Bletchley Park before 1977; and as my time there coincided with a passionate first love and marriage, a natural delicacy forbade me to speak during the lifetime of the man (himself a prisoner of war, and an evader) to whom subsequently I was very happily married for 34 years. For my tale embraces also the shared and diverse experiences of two young people who loved each other and who grew to maturity in the forcing-house of the war. Perhaps more than usually naïve and innocent undergraduates of the late 1930s, we were hammered on the anvil of national challenge into characters of realism, responsibility and resolution. I believe that in the personal is reflected a universal experience of the times. Moreover, within these particular biographies unfold two further enigmas – of character and destiny, and of fate.

There is an increasing public awareness of Ultra, and equally of the Special Air Service Regiment in which my first husband latterly served, and in which he met his death in circumstances still unexplained. Transcendent in this book is my desire to carve some modest memorial to one who has no real memorial. Leslie Cairns's short adult life was a counterpoint of love and war. I had the honour to be the object of that love. If I am accused of unblushing candour in quoting extensively from intimate correspondence, my justification must be that the man himself is his best biographer, and that his letters interpret his character and its development – from something little more than a schoolboy to that of a seasoned officer in the special forces – far more truly than could any words of mine.

It has seemed to me that a memoir which relates both to the intelligence community at Bletchley Park and also to the SAS may not be without general interest – albeit that the Special Air Service of the Second World War had a very different character and image from that acquired by the regiment today; and that the recent rash of sensational peacetime revelations by MI5 officers has little in common with this attempt to offer a portrait – a period piece – of the innocent aspects of wartime intelligence duties.

This story reflects two utterly different yet complementary aspects of the war-effort: the cerebral and cloistered, and the physical (though far from unthinking) and perilous. In his preface to Winterbotham's *The Ultra Secret*, Marshal of the Royal Air Force Sir John Slessor made this observation: 'To all those who have been brought up in the belief that the Allied victory over the Fascist powers was accomplished by the superior force of arms and strategy, perhaps this book will provide the sobering thought that it almost didn't happen. Let the reader judge for himself just how much the near miracle of Ultra helped to make victory possible.' The danger inherent in much of the fascinating revelations about Ultra, however, is that of being carried away on the crest of a wave of intellectual achievement. No matter how incalculable an advantage Ultra gave us, its successful application in action depended upon the tactical ability of the field commander and the dogged courage of the regimental soldier, whether he be in a regular or an irregular unit. In a memorial service to honour the SAS and other volunteer special forces, held in Westminster Abbey on 21 May 1948, Winston Churchill spoke thus: 'We may feel sure that nothing of which we have any knowledge and record has ever been done by mortal men which surpasses the splendour and daring of their feats of arms.'

★ ★ ★

I am writing these words on the fiftieth anniversary of the start of the greatest and most justifiable of all wars; and this book will be published 50 years on from that year which ranks as one of the most evocative in British history, symbolising as it does the spirit of an age in which the nation found greatness, and countless ordinary people were ennobled by selfless and heroic deeds.

Irene Young
September 1989

PROLOGUE

Adventuring was new to me. It began in Disraeli's own county of Buckinghamshire, and with this letter: 'You should attend for duty at Bletchley Park, Bletchley, on Monday 21st September. On arrival at Bletchley Station you should telephone from the post office in the station yard to Bletchley 320, extension 309, and ask the Transport Officer for instructions.'

It was September 1942, and I was sitting apprehensively in the train from London as it snaked slowly through the dull North Bucks countryside. With disappointment I had watched the landscape change from the leafy beech woods of the Chilterns to the monotony of the flat, featureless brickfields. Presently the train halted, and I strained anxiously to hear the guard call out 'Bletchley!'; for since the threat of invasion all signposts and names of towns at the roadside or on the railway had been removed or obliterated. *The Times* of 31 March 1940 had jauntily commented that 'citizens wandering off the beaten track will be able to experience the exhilarating feeling of being explorers'. I was in fact to be one of the last of those innocent explorers, for within a month or so, with the turn of our fortunes in North Africa and the diminishing threat to this island, it was thought safe to lift the veil of obscurity from the face of Britain.

I had travelled from my home in Scotland to London, that in itself something of an adventure for one brought up in the narrower pre-war world, and I had there caught a train back northwards to Bletchley. Like most people at the time who lived beyond the immediate locality, I had never heard of the place; nor did I know (as indeed I could not have known) that in this drab and ugly town was concealed one of the nerve-centres of the Allied war-effort. For at Bletchley – chosen because it was only an hour's train journey from London, and on the line equidistant between Oxford and Cambridge, those catchment areas for brilliant mathematicians and chess-players, and equally for distinguished academics who could turn their talents and scholarly precision to a more immediate purpose – was located 'Station X', the Government Code and Cypher School, recently renamed with deliberate ambiguity Government Communications Headquarters, where the German Enigma code, the 'Ultra Secret', was being broken.

I got down from the train, found the telephone box and, with thudding heart, rang the given number. A crisp voice answered with instructions to wait. I waited. I waited uneasily for about 40 minutes. Then, timidly, I rang again, and again I waited, with mounting anxiety. What should I do, I thought, wildly irrational, if I were just *left* here? I did not know where Bletchley Park was, nor what I had been appointed to do there. As with all recruits to the forces, and civilians posted (as I had just been) to a government department intimately connected with the conduct of the war, and of which the bland title suggested concealment of its real function, I realised I was there 'for the duration'. I had no idea of conditions of service, nor when I should ever be allowed to go home again. As time passed with no response to my telephone call, the defiant spirit of adventure with which I had set off that morning began to evaporate:

> I, a stranger and afraid
> In a world I never made.

After what seemed an eternity of apprehension, a jeep appeared, driven by an army sergeant who called out my name. What in the world was *he* doing here?, I thought, in my innocence. I had been appointed to what they called the Country Section of the Foreign Office, and I do believe I expected a sleek motor-car to meet me!

My road to Bletchley Park wound back beyond the last few weeks, when I had graduated from Edinburgh University; back beyond the previous six months, when I had broken my engagement to a young man I still loved dearly; back, indeed, as far as 1937, which is the true beginning of this triple-stranded story of Enigma.

CHAPTER 1

Gaudeamus igitur
Iuvenes dum sumus . . .
MEDIEVAL STUDENTS' SONG, C.1250

I went up to Edinburgh University by way of a strange and fractured education. It began at a convent of the Ursuline Order, where I learned French and the omnipresence of sin. Then I attended a small private school which failed, the remaining pupils being transferred to another establishment where lack of discipline almost totally occluded learning. From this I was removed at my own request. This may sound priggish, but I was on the verge of intellectual awakening, which in my case far preceded emotional development, and I realised that I needed greater stimulus than had hitherto been available to me.

I was sent then as a day-girl to Esdaile, a school founded originally to give the daughters of the Scottish clergy the academic education which could previously be afforded only for the sons of the manse. As such, it was the oldest girls' private school in Scotland. Here, for the first time, I was made to work. It was 1933 – the year I bought an autographed copy of Vera Brittain's *Testament of Youth*; the year Hitler came to power.

The headmistress under whose régime I laboured was a disciplinarian of the Victorian kind. One of the assistant mistresses later told me that the staff, too, were sternly governed, and their free time – very little in this boarding-school which demanded many evening duties – severely censored. If, for example, they were going to a concert or to an improving lecture, then an egg would be left for their late supper; more frivolous entertainment earned no rations. This gratuity was nicknamed 'The Intellectual Egg'. The husband of

17

my closest friend from those days later dubbed Esdaile 'the school at Lowood'. And yet there was an extremely happy family relationship between the staff and pupils, united in sympathy under this stern authority.

I had cherished an immaturely extravagant ambition to be a Shakespearean actress but, in spite of having gained first-class merit certificates at the British Empire Shakespeare Society festivals, and having taken part in a public theatre production, I realised, mercifully, that I had far from sufficient talent. I remained, however, the school's principal *diseuse*, and was called upon to perform at entertainments such as those put on for the annual visit of the Lord High Commissioner to the General Assembly of the Church of Scotland. This was literally a State occasion for, as the representative of the Crown, the Lord High Commissioner is accorded royal honours. His Grace would arrive at the gates of Esdaile, his limousine flying the Scottish royal banner, accompanied by his suite – Purse Bearer, Chaplain, ADCs and Ladies-in-Waiting. What mattered most to the girls was whether he would remember to grant the customary day's holiday: we had no such thing as a half-term holiday because pupils from remote parishes could not afford to travel home for such a short period, but during Assembly week, when many of the parents were in Edinburgh, a family reunion could be relished.

At the end of my first year at Esdaile, John Buchan held the office of Lord High Commissioner for the second time. I was chosen to recite a dreadful monologue in which I had to assume a phoney American accent. This had been rehearsed so often in front of the whole school that I was thoroughly embarrassed by it, but His Grace kindly restored some self-respect to me by shouting out 'Well done!'. I remember yet John Buchan's exhortation to the girls that afternoon – that we should pursue 'ideal aims, business methods and sporting spirit'. On this occasion, too, Buchan's sister Anna (the novelist O. Douglas), who was acting as Lady-in-Waiting to Her Grace, also addressed us. The gist of her speech was of homely comfort: 'Don't worry if you are not too clever. Just write books, like me.' The next year, when the (late) Duke of Kent held the office, I narrowly missed a *real* Royal Command performance because the weather was fine and the alternative outdoor gymnastic and dance programme was presented. By this time, however, my mind was turning towards English literature. It was a natural inclination, fostered by an inspiring teacher, and I began filling the school magazine with poetry, influenced only too obviously by Keats and Tennyson.

When I was 16, the school appointed a new headmistress, Mrs Dorothy Calembert, who had considerable influence on my later adolescent years. She was the unlikely daughter of a Church of Scotland missionary to Rajputana, and was charming, brilliant, and unconventional. For all her genuine Christian piety, she had a delightfully broad and humorous attitude to religion. She had married a Belgian Catholic (an official of the Belgian air ministry, subsequently killed in the R101 airship disaster), and had refused to raise her only daughter in the Faith, which, in those less liberal days, showed considerable courage. She taught us Religious Education, and I always remember the essay which she set for the sixth form – 'Thoughts on the Holy Ghost' – quite the most difficult subject I had tackled! She remarked on returning our painful efforts: 'When I think of the Holy Ghost I always think of a stack of books in the attic, because my grandfather wrote a book on the Holy Ghost and it didn't sell'; and all the clergy daughters delighted in her irreverence.

In my last year I was elected a prefect, and I can still recall Mrs Calembert's words at the ceremony of installation. She was a sympathiser with the Oxford Group movement, and was also a pacifist. 'I belong,' she said, 'to what the French call *La Génération Perdue*. We watched our brothers and our boyfriends go off to war. Some of them never came back; others came back wounded. We *let* them do it to us!' (I can still hear the crescendo in her voice). 'You must *never* let them do it to you! And that is why I am glad to see you exercising a wise choice today, for I trust that in the years to come you will exercise a wise choice in matters of your country.' Mrs Calembert's brother-in-law, Charles Judd, was then Chief Education Officer of the League of Nations Union – he was later to be Secretary and Director-General – and we were all enrolled in the League, and wore on our gym-tunics the blue-and-gold badge with its symbolic map of the world, that world in which all peoples were supposed to live at peace for ever. Mrs Calembert frequently put to us the case for disarmament, and though I admired her 'on this side idolatry', I could not, unlike so many of my schoolfellows, go along with her in this. I felt very strongly that the way to stop this dreadful Herr Hitler was to be powerful enough to act as policeman among the nations.

★ ★ ★

On a morning early in October 1937 I crept into the First Ordinary Latin class in the Old College of the University of Edinburgh – Latin was a required subject for several Arts degrees. No fanfare of welcome then, nor any Freshers' Week easing us into this challenging new world. I took my place among some 200 others in the old-fashioned lecture-theatre, where the desks were scarred with the names of generations of students, and the seats steeply raked and narrow enough to keep us uncomfortably awake.

Three days later I found myself at a Freshers' dance organised by the University Conservative Association in the Women's Union at 54 George Square. I had not been over-eager to go. As an only child, educated at girls' schools, I was rather shy of boys; besides, I was set on a career, and did not favour the possibility of any romantic distractions. I was, however, over-persuaded by a friend. On what casual decisions hang the great significances of our lives!

For this event I had needed a new evening dress – my first proper ball-gown. My mother came with me to the shop (while we were 'dependants', our parents bought our clothes in those days) and she decided that the dress would be taffeta, as this material would be hard-wearing and would not *tear* easily. (I myself yearned for floating silk chiffon, but taffeta it was.) I failed to know what my mother, who was very trusting and liberal with me, thought I should be getting up to, and with what ravening young men! The dress we eventually chose shaded from pale to midnight blue, had a demure neckline, a stitched belt – and puff sleeves! I was the archetypal Girl in the Alice-Blue Gown of the current popular song. Clothes acquired during the many years since then have been discarded when outworn or out of fashion, but that dress, limp and faded, still hangs, memorially, in my wardrobe.

After a few dances I was approached by a dark-haired, slightly built young man, wearing a dress doublet and a kilt of Macdonald tartan. I noted his velvet-dark eyes and his engaging smile, but these particulars did not register as strongly as the fact that here was someone easy to talk to, with whom I did not have to *make* conversation; there seemed no need of any self-consciousness or artifice. We danced and talked together for the remainder of the evening. He told me that his name was Leslie Cairns and that he was reading History. Like myself, he was an only child. He had been destined for Oxford, but when his father died the previous year that had become financially impossible – in those days there were no government grants – and his mother had moved from Stirling, where he had been born, and had settled in Edinburgh so that he might attend university. He discovered that I was reading English, and when he asked about the particular classes I was taking, I was too naïve and too unaware of myself to see any significance in the question. At midnight, obedient to my parents' instruction, I left the ball in a taxi, thinking what a pleasant interlude it had been, and that if all people were as friendly, then university was going to be an agreeable social as well as intellectual experience.

The following Monday, when I came out of my 12 o'clock class in Minto House, there was the same young man assiduously studying the noticeboard in the hall. After greeting me with well-feigned surprise, he suggested that as we lived on the same side of town we might walk home together. And so, all resolution to be solely a career-girl thrown to the winds, there began a love-affair, menaced, like so many, by the gathering storm. Much later I remarked to Leslie that I had not, that first night, been conscious of any destiny. 'I was,' he replied. 'You should have seen me going home. The fellow I was with must have wondered what was the matter with me. I left him to do all the talking; I fell over my own feet, and I burned myself with my cigarette . . .'

* * *

At first we behaved like the couple of children we were – he was 17 and I a year older. We talked interminably, laughed euphorically, and teased one another without mercy. Life (if Hitler allowed) was going to be a great adventure; and one of our stock jokes was Leslie's schoolboy ambition to be Viceroy of India!

ENIGMA VARIATIONS

We queued for 'the gods' in the theatre, and when the doors opened we would rush headlong up the steep stairs, overtaking, where we could, those ahead of us, in order to secure good seats. We saved our scant pocket-money for university balls, and dressed up, and rode eight to a taxi, ending up in the small hours at the coffee stall at the Mound. In those days a dance (unlike disco dancing) provided a thrilling opportunity for physical contact during the delicate early stages of a relationship. We went in the party of the Dean of the Faculty of Medicine to one such ball, held in aid of the University Settlement. It was an affair both decorous and 'dry', but the end of the evening was considerably enlivened by the (very) late arrival of the Dean's inebriated son, the future poet Sydney Goodsir Smith who, brandishing a whisky bottle, kept shouting aggressively 'God save the Duke of Windsor!' during the singing of the national anthem which always ended such events. However, since most of us lived on very modest allowances from our parents, such grand balls were in the nature of a rare treat, and our regular pleasures were of a much humbler order. Fourpence took us to the local cinema, and again for fourpence we could sit for a whole Saturday morning in Mackie's, Princes Street, with a live orchestra as accompaniment to our coffee and endless conversation.

In the spring of 1938, along with two of Leslie's old schoolfellows, we visited the Empire Exhibition – that last explosion of confidence before the Empire's martyrdom and final dissolution. Leslie and I rode to Glasgow in the dickey of the only motor-car in the possession of any of our university friends. It was an exciting and carefree day out. We marvelled at the daring innovation of Tait's Tower and the spectacular national shows presented by each of the dominions and colonies. I was particularly impressed by the gracious and beautiful Dutch gabling of the South African pavilion. I was not to foresee, at this time when far travel was a scarcely considered dream, that within ten years I should, as a holder of a South African passport and in a world totally altered, be admiring the architecture in the original at Constantia in the Cape. We stopped at the representation of a Highland clachan, and had the blacksmith make for each of us a miniature lucky horseshoe with the date 1938 stamped upon it. On my desk I have mine still.

Of course, like all young people we were desperate to put the world to rights, and were deeply concerned at the growing might of Nazi Germany. One of my friends had been sent to a German finishing-school, and I was perturbed and shocked when I discovered that she had returned home indoctrinated with National Socialism. Then, too, I had undertaken to look after a German student, Gertrud Vieting, in my English literature class: I was horrified at her anti-semitism and her worship of the Führer and all that he stood for. She had completed her period of conscription in the Labour Service in Germany, and was spending some time in Britain in order to improve her English. With extraordinary prescience, she was planning on her return home to study Russian and Japanese in order to become an interpreter. The preparedness for war throughout German society seemed in marked contrast to the atmosphere in the University of Edinburgh where there was a distinct element of pacifism, and where even the OTC appeared to spend a disproportionate time on the organisation of dances rather than on field days. Gertrud went back to Germany early in 1938, and we kept in touch until the Munich crisis, when I decided not to continue with the correspondence. She had three brothers, and the family lived in Gelsenkirchen in the Ruhr; I often wondered what happened to them.

During the period 1937–8 various organisations in the city and the university began to hold rallies or services of intercession in support of Christian dissidents in Germany. Pastors from the German Lutheran Confession Church addressed meetings in the university, explaining the plight of those of their brethren who on account of their opposition to Hitler had been sent to concentration camps. The most notable of these was Martin Niemöller who between 1937, when I went up to university, and the start of the war, was something of a *cause célèbre*. He had been a U-boat commander in the First World War and a loyal and patriotic German, but found himself unable to accept the doctrines of National Socialism. He was incarcerated until 1945. Dietrich Bonhoeffer was less fortunate, and was executed that same year. After his release Niemöller pronounced the words that have become famous:

First they came for the Jews, and I did not speak out, for I was not a Jew. Then they came for the communists, and I did not speak out, for I was not a communist. Then they came for the trade unionists, and I did not speak out, for I was not a trade unionist. And then they came for me, and there was no one to speak out for me.

These words were a retrospective reproach to all those in Europe who out of self-delusion or cowardice had turned a blind eye to what was happening within Germany.

But now, in 1938, these meetings made clear to us students that the German concentration camps were not a figment of the British propaganda machine, as some wished to believe. For our part, Leslie and I had begun to realise that Britain would have at last to stand up to Hitler, even if it meant war.

A tremor shook our happiness.

★ ★ ★

Our conversation, Leslie's and mine, ranged over all manner of topics, from politics to philosophy, from heraldry to humanism. We were both *talkers*. Never before had I encountered a mind so sympathetic to my own, nor a humour so compatible. Leslie's optimism countered the pessimism which was inherent in my psychology. We were, I think, of the same physical type, though he was dark and I tawny-haired, with grey-blue eyes. Once or twice we were taken for brother and sister, which greatly amused and delighted Leslie. He was not, strictly speaking, handsome, if that is to be tall and powerfully built; but his luminous dark eyes and very white teeth, and his sensuous mouth counteracted by a firm chin, were enough for him to be considered 'good-looking'. His nature was deep but uncomplicated, genuine, passionate yet balanced; he had a keen intelligence and was dubbed 'effortlessly bright'. Interested in innumerable subjects, he fell short, I think, of the truly scholarly. *People* were of primary importance to him, and he had a quick perception of and delight in the quirks and oddities of human behaviour. He had a lively humour – humour, perhaps, rather than wit – sweet to medium-dry; a portion of wit, too, was his, but he had not lived long enough for it to be sharpened by disillusionment. Friends observed that whenever he entered a room everyone's spirits rose: beguiling encomium!

Though we walked home together every day, within the university we lived independent lives. Never once did we share a class. Leslie was a member of the Philomathic Society, which was a junior rival to the famous Speculative Society ('The Spec'), which élite debating society he might well, in time, have joined and revelled in its splendid traditions and its associations with Scott, Jeffrey, Cockburn, Stevenson and the literary luminaries of Edinburgh. He fenced, and he was also in the OTC. Incidentally, the Battery, which was the unit he joined, had ceased to be a mounted battery only as recently as the academic year before we went up to university: at its annual camps it had trained with six-horse teams. And even in Leslie's day the uniform remained antiquated; I well remember his struggles with his puttees, just such as were worn in the First World War.

For my part, I belonged to the Student Christian Movement – a legacy of Esdaile – and to the choral section of the Musical Society, which during my first term took part in a play performed by the Indian students. I had the complicated delight of putting on a sari in an atmosphere heady with sandalwood. I also contributed to *The Student*, the undergraduate literary magazine, with the same zeal as, but with only slightly more originality, than I had to the school magazine. Most of us wrote under pseudonyms. With conscious self-deprecation I chose that of Icarus, and I envied the talent of two of my senior contemporaries in particular – Sagramore (Ian Robertson) and Aucassin (Charles McAra).

Summer brought walks on Blackford Hill and the Pentlands; not for us was the privacy of flats or cars. How simple our pleasures were, how innocent ourselves! Yet, underneath this artless friendship there ran, unacknowledged, a current of deep emotion. We had no qualifications, no money, no 'prospects'; we were both absurdly young, but the Munich crisis of September 1938 forced from Leslie a 'declaration'. He was holidaying in Oban with a school friend; I came home from the ghoulish voluntary task of assembling gas-masks, and was feeling anguished and depressed. Waiting for me was this letter:

I have never had the courage to tell you this. It may sound

strange coming from a loud-mouthed specimen like me, but I am shy, and now I am writing what I would a thousand times have preferred to tell you, but hadn't the courage. We have discussed many topics (and teased one another to death), but we have never touched on the subject of love. Perhaps you think I am too young to know anything about it, but you will be wrong. Somehow I dislike showing my emotions, which are very real, so you may have thought I was a flippant sort of creature, never bothering my head about anything serious. I wish you could see me now, in a blue funk and my pen dithering about in my fingers. I am terribly afraid this letter may offend you. If it does, don't read any further, and burn the thing – I won't think the worse of you. I love you, Irene, and now I've written it, I feel quite strange – a funny sort of sensation which I've never had before; but then, I've never said or written such a thing. I am only a schoolboy, as you truly remark, but what I'm saying is true (and I've no string in my pocket nowadays!) . . . And now I must sleep (if I can). I expect things [the international situation] will be clear when I see you.

I was deeply moved by this ingenuous, stumbling confession – touched and happy, and proud as though I had been awarded the Order of Merit! But the diffident, sceptical part of me was afraid, perhaps not unnaturally, that a boy's love would be volatile like a beautiful butterfly. How wrong I was.

CHAPTER 2

How horrible, fantastic, incredible it is that
we should be digging trenches and trying on gas
masks here because of a quarrel in a far-away
country between people of whom we know nothing.
NEVILLE CHAMBERLAIN, BROADCAST ON 27 SEPTEMBER 1938

These words of Chamberlain must seem unbelievable to the present generation now that the world has so shrunk and it is a truism that no man is an island. From Germany Gertrud Vieting wrote to me in what was to be our last exchange:

> Those days have been a dreadful and great sorrow for everybody. There was no enthusiasm wherever you went to, but when at last newspapers and wireless announced the peaceable solution, there was no limit for enthusiasm and joy. I often went to the cinema to see at least some pictures of those historical days . . . I also saw the arrival of the great statesmen in their own countries and the tremendous demonstrations with which their peoples greeted them – now the crisis has gone we all realised how much all our doing had been influenced by it.

Of course both the nature of the international situation and of my relationship with Leslie were now changed. We were each relieved that the Munich crisis had been resolved, though we were ashamed of our relief; and we knew that despite Chamberlain's naïve optimism, it was only a respite. War now seemed inevitable. Nevertheless, we rejoiced in our newly admitted love.

When we were apart, as we sometimes were in the university vacations, we rarely used the telephone, so I had many letters to cherish. Leslie never 'composed' a letter; it was always 'Look in thy heart and write', and I agreed with Donne that 'Still more than kisses letters mingle souls'.

I had been brought up in a family in which affection, though it was certainly not lacking, was not openly shown; where the old Scots adage, 'Dinna get above yersel', so well intentioned as an antidote to *hubris*, tended to blight any growing self-confidence. Leslie's was the first love that nourished that confidence. His buoyancy lifted my spirit; his humour, his warmth and open approval, let the sunlight into my life and flooded the whole world with a new radiance. I had always possessed a surface social ease, but underneath, well concealed, lay a chasm of diffidence and reserve. This may have been due to my family background, or to my convent years. Also I had a brilliant cousin whose talents everyone, especially my father, openly revered. I think I can honestly say that I did not resent this, and, indeed, joined in the admiration, but the circumstance did not increase my self-esteem. I feared to give myself away, to trust; and Leslie suffered for it. He wrote at this time about the difficulty of convincing me of his devotion:

> If I weren't naturally optimistic, you would drive me to despair. I miss you whenever I'm out of your sight. I want you more than anything and it positively hurts me; not because what I *want* is out of the question – that would be merely sulky – but because I *need* you. I really do. I see you in every book I open. When I look at a picture of a woman, I think, 'She's not as beautiful as Irene'. I can always remember the scent you use, the way you walk, the shape of your hands. You are before my eyes as I write – head slightly cocked, expressing a gentle scepticism; but your eyes have something despite of the mask you wear. Perhaps I will be able to remove the mask, and the 'something' will blossom. Oh, darling, please believe and trust, and let it blossom. You never worry me as I do you, but for all that, I have my cross to bear and it never lets up much.

I was also absurdly idealistic, and my insecurity demanded total perfection as its sacrifice; and, for one not naturally patient, Leslie bore the yoke with commendable forbearance. From Inverness he wrote in the Easter vacation of 1939:

> I had a lovely run today, with a carriage to myself as far as Pitlochry. There were millions(!) of lambs, and a young billy-goat tried to race the train, and bumped into a fence. I do wish you had been with me, for I've never seen a more living countryside. It was really spring, everything bursting with life, trees budding, men ploughing, and a crate of hens in Aviemore nearly lifted the roof off the station. I've seemed never to notice the world around me so acutely – always as a background only. My darling, I missed you. I wanted you there to see everything, to sit opposite me and let me look at you. I felt so odd, most of the way – bits of poetry running through my head. There was a sombre little loch outside Perth that 'whistled stiff and dry about the marge' and I half expected to see an arm clothed in white samite come out of the water. I expect you think I'm dotty, but, upon my word, it's true. And how I wanted you there, Irene; sometimes it gives me an ache, but not often as it did today . . . My dear, please remember that I love you beyond all things. It nearly shatters me sometimes. And I don't want much back – just a little love of *myself*, and not a shining knight with my face. Darling, I do try hard to come up to your expectations – in many ways you have bent considerably towards my views; that's as it should be. But, more than that, I love *you* – the real you, body and soul. I, too, have had my dream of a perfect lady, better than a princess. Well, I've found her in you – and you are far, far more than she ever was – you're *real*, and so beautiful. Yet I think of you with as much reverence as I ever thought of her. There are many things I would like to say, but I am shy – please believe that; and so I try to let my looks and such things speak for me. Oh, my love, you must never think that I would even touch you casually. When I hold you in my arms you really do make me feel weak in a

funny kind of way – as if nothing existed but you and me. When you knock yourself in any way, I feel as though I've hurt myself. I even seem to think sometimes as though I were inside your mind. Please don't be offended with anything I've said, my dear; this letter has got beyond my control and rambled on too much . . .

I am sure I did not deserve such a rich outpouring of unconditional love. Perhaps I came nearer to deserving it much later, when I had learned to trust it, and later still, when I had suffered for it; but not then, not then!

During another absence, Leslie wrote: 'Dear girl, I have begun to miss you already . . . I love you beyond words, more than any mortal soul. Sometimes it gives me an ache . . . a sort of pain mixed with joy . . .' And to this day it is 'joy' that springs to mind when I think of Leslie. He possessed a quality such as I can describe only as 'brilliant innocence', a passionate, childlike delight in simple, everyday things, which he invested with glamour and magic, evoking latent responses in me. He was *too* happy, *too* buoyant, *too* loving of life. He had a sort of 'fatality' about him (to use Masefield's phrase in his *Letters from the Front*). I thought so then; and when war broke out, I knew it.

Like most well brought-up young people of the time, we did not care to show our feelings in public, and were very circumspect; but the current ran between us, and we noticed that people looked at us with a sort of envious tenderness, and, later, when Leslie was in uniform, so young and imperilled, with pity also.

★ ★ ★

As the year wore on and the war seemed inevitable, Leslie spoke of his probable role in it. As I have said, he was in the University Battery of the Officers' Training Corps, and it would be in the Royal Artillery in which he would serve. 'I'm afraid of not acquitting myself well,' he said one day, 'that I shan't be able to give a man the order to fire. I could do it myself, but I might not be able to tell another to . . . I'm afraid, not of dying, because then I won't know about it . . . but of coming back in pieces . . . I wouldn't mind having a leg off, because then I could still work, but I've a horror of being blind!' I found such sentiments unbearably distressing. Both of us were equivocal about our belief in an afterlife, but clung to the comforting thought of it. Leslie said he would come back to me even if he had to 'argue with the Almighty and beg for leave of absence'! But even this banter gave me a terrible pang.

Though a grandson of the manse, Leslie was not particularly religious, but he often went to church to please his mother. After one such dutiful attendance, he quoted to me Violet Jacob's 'Tam i' the Kirk':

> O Jean, my Jean, when the bell ca's the congregation
> O'er valley and hill wi' the ding frae its iron mou';
> When a'body's thochts is set on their ain salvation,
> Mine's set on you.
>
> There's a reid rose on the Buik o' the Word afore ye
> That was growin' braw on its bush at the keek o' day
> But that lad that pu'd yon flower i' the mornin's glory –
> He canna pray.
>
> He canna pray, but there's nane i' the kirk will heed him
> Whaur he sits sae still his lane at the side o' the wa',
> For nane but the reid rose kens what my lassie gied him –
> It and us twa.
>
> He canna sing for the sang that his ain hairt raises,
> He canna see for the mist that's afore his e'en,
> And a voice drouns the hale o' the psalms and the paraphrases,
> Crying 'Jean, Jean, Jean!'

I did not know the poem, and was delighted with it. We both loved poetry, and certain verses came to have especial significance for us, not for their literary quality only, but for reasons of occasion or of sentiment. Such were the Marquis of Montrose's 'My Dear and Only Love', W.B. Yeats's 'Aedh Wishes for the Cloths of Heaven', and many of the poems of A.E. Housman, whose preoccupation with soldiers and death, and the poignant use of irony and meiosis, gave his poetry an epigrammatic and an elegiac quality according with the times, and with our mood. And, of course, there was Rupert Brooke (unjustly considered unfashionable today), whose tutor at King's College, Cambridge, had been Oliffe Richmond, my Professor of Humanity at Edinburgh. Richmond was reported to display great sensitivity when reading Latin poetry, but I remember him only for what I then considered a dry, scholarly preoccupation with establishing the exact location of Virgil's birthplace by means of measurements in Roman water-mileage.

Leslie enjoyed music, and often played my father's piano. He had a small talent, but a sensitive touch – I recollect Liszt's *Consolation No. 2* being one of his favourite pieces. Later, in the army, he derived great comfort from attending the concerts which proliferated everywhere as an antidote to war. After attending, as a cadet, one such concert in Leeds, Leslie reported: 'We had a ruinous day . . . had lunch in an hotel, two tables away from J.B. Priestley who spoke at the concert, and I felt quite like something out of a society or notables gossip column. But really, he is a most repulsive man to look at, though an excellent talker.' I was very interested, as Priestley was a great celebrity on account of his 'Postscripts' – wireless talks after the news on Sundays. These were very morale-boosting, and had been designed as an antidote to the propaganda pouring out of Germany from 'Lord Haw Haw' (the Irishman, William Joyce). Counting his broadcasts to the United States, the BBC reckoned that Priestley had the biggest listening audience in the world; so perhaps his appearance did not matter so much.

I was not as musical as Leslie; I played no instrument, but I used to sing – I had had a few lessons, and had even won a music festival competition – and 'One Fine Day' from *Madame Butterfly* was the star piece in my repertoire. My father, a trained amateur singer who was well-known in Edinburgh for his charity concerts, used, in the fashion of the time, to hold musical evenings at home, and I sometimes sang it then. I am not sure if Leslie was ever present, but he certainly connected me with the aria. Young people seemed to be much more integrated with their families then, and I spent many a happy Sunday afternoon at Leslie's home when his mother gave tea-parties for young cousins and friends. She enjoyed the company of the young, and we always felt at ease with her. Likewise, Leslie was often at my house, and I believe my mother really loved him – perhaps as the son she never had. He could certainly charm older ladies without really trying.

Throughout the last university session, the essential seriousness of the international crisis struck home. The ranks of the OTC were swelled by an increase in the number of recruits. More candidates than ever were taking Certificates A and B. The last number of *The Student* for the session 1938–9 contained this passage at the end of its OTC Notes section:

> There is no doubt that within recent years the OTC has become a vaguely unpopular and rather misunderstood organisation; a thing apart from university life, the refuge of a few misguided enthusiasts, amiable Philistines, and more than a few 'good-time Charlies'. All this was, in view of the spirit of the times, understandable if disheartening, and substantially untrue. But now, as in the outside world, the scales have fallen and perspective has been readjusted.

★ ★ ★

In the summer vacation of 1939, ever ready for adventure, Leslie signed on as a deckhand on a cargo-boat sailing from Grangemouth to the ports of Sweden. He used to spend his scant pocket-money on trinkets for me, brooches and pendants, and sometimes little things with a whimsical touch – a Chinese painted leaf, an ivory egg half an inch long which opened to reveal a microscopic chicken. And now, from Stockholm's Crown jeweller (always he liked to do things in style) he brought me the finest gold chain I had ever seen, and on it a pendant, a small silver-gilt replica of the Swedish Royal Arms – quite sophisticated taste, I thought, for a boy of nineteen.

'I don't think I could ever be a sailor,' he wrote, 'though it is fine for a change. You are away too long . . . if you see what I mean!' Then, referring to my Doubting Thomas nature: 'I do hope you haven't forgotten all I've said *when I am not there to say it.*'

Had the voyage been a few weeks later, Leslie might have been interned in Sweden, and I should be telling quite a different story. As it was, he returned home to mounting international crisis, and the world as we knew it about to be swept away for ever.

CHAPTER 3

Once only by the garden gate
Our lips were joined and parted.
I must fulfil an empty fate
And travel the uncharted.

Hail and farewell! I must arise,
Leave here the fatted cattle,
And paint on foreign lands and skies
My Odyssey of battle.

The tented Kosmos my abode,
I press, a wilful stranger:
My mistress still the open road
And the bright eyes of danger.

R.L. STEVENSON: 'YOUTH AND LOVE'

On 1 September 1939, the day Poland was invaded, and two days before Britain declared war on Germany, Leslie volunteered for military service. Of course, with our views on Hitler and National Socialism, I was prepared for him to be willingly involved – in theory. In actuality, I had not expected that he would offer himself so soon. I found that I was mortally afraid; first, naturally, that he would be killed; secondly, that I should lose this magical relationship that had transformed my life. Henceforth Leslie would inhabit a world I could not share. I feared that he would change; that his values would alter; that the warm, sensitive boy I knew would become distanced and hardened. Out of this fear and resentment I taunted him with all the repertoire of the war poetry on which we had both been reared, such as Newbolt's 'The Volunteer':

He lept to arms unbidden,
Unneeded, overbold.
His face by earth is hidden,
His heart in earth is cold.

Curse on that reckless daring
That could not wait the call,
The proud fantastic bearing
That would be first to fall!

As a bitter Parthian shot I ended with the lines from Lovelace,

I cou'd not love thee, Dear, so much
Loved I not honour more . . .

which in their evocation of a past age of chivalry and derring-do seemed to match both the cavalier spirit of romantic and traditional young men, and the lot of their women, through the ages, who waited and wept.

Leslie did not retaliate. He knew well enough that there had been a spur of excitement to his action; but there was also moral purpose and simple patriotism. He had been educated at a small public school – Newstead at Doune, now no more – where 'King and Country' was still a valid cause. Besides, he believed he would be opposing a great evil. From his mother, brought up in a Banffshire manse, and graduating in 1902 as one of Scotland's earliest women doctors, he had inherited high courage and a sense of adventure and of duty. A certain intrepidity must have descended from his clergyman grandfather who insisted on visiting his sick parishioners, no matter how virulent their diseases, and on whose death the town of Macduff renamed his church after him – the Gardner Memorial. A strain of valour, too, may have filtered down from a great-uncle who had been a brigadier-general, and from a second cousin who was an air-ace in the First World War and who had had the distinction of being shot down by Richthofen.

I soon grew ashamed of my outburst and tried hard to see Leslie's point of view. As it turned out, the army would not accept him until his twentieth birthday – for the very good reason that there was neither organisation nor equipment to cope with more than a limited number of recruits. Indeed, when he did at last report at the Uniacke Barracks at Harrogate, he found that the 'gun' on which he had to do his basic training and learn 'the naming of parts' was a Heath Robinson affair with a barrel made from a length of iron pipe, a rude timber carriage with cartwheels, and a limber consisting of a pair of rubber tyres and a water butt. This ludicrous contraption, which might have been created in a children's adventure playground, was christened by the gunners 'Auld Bella'.

I have said that Leslie's character was uncomplicated, but there was one enigma at the heart of it. He was more than usually avid of life, yet he was prepared to hazard it before he was called upon to do so. It was as if his zest for living encompassed even the risk of dying. He loved me deeply and cared greatly for my happiness, yet he was drawn to actions which inevitably caused me distress. This dichotomy – sensitivity, love and life, versus daring, duty and death – seemed to approximate to the ancient code of chivalry, and to recall the spirit of 1914. My inability to come to terms with this enigma once nearly destroyed our happiness and, ironically, my eventual acceptance may have destroyed it finally.

Meanwhile, we returned to university, and tried to carry on as before. But neither of us had much stomach for academic life; it had suddenly lost its relevance. Previously, as well as being an enjoyable enrichment of life, it had been seen as a preparation for our future. What future was there now? This was the period of the 'phoney war' and, in practical terms, the chief inconveniences were the blackout and the carrying of gas-masks everywhere; even to go without one across the Quad to the lavatory was to risk a ticking-off from the university staff. The blackout, indeed, could be more than a mere nuisance. One night, walking in the city centre, my father suddenly found himself sprawling on his back. As he recovered his senses, he heard, fading into the darkness, voices exclaiming, 'What was that?' He had been totally invisible to two burly men coming towards him from the opposite direction.

In April came the invasion of Norway – three days after Chamberlain had made his fatuous remark that Hitler had 'missed the bus'. Leslie fretted and fumed at the delay in his call-up, and his eagerness to be off smote me to the heart. He had orders to join a Royal Artillery training regiment at Harrogate for a period of three months in the ranks during which he would be assessed as a potential officer. (Having been a member of a university OTC and having obtained Certificates A and B, he was, of course, marked down for a commission, but his probationary period had to precede eventual selection for a formal course at an Officer Cadet Training Unit – an OCTU.) The night before he eventually left for Harrogate, we were at a university dance, anodyne against the parting. It was 10 May 1940, and the band was suddenly stopped while over the wireless came the news that Chamberlain had resigned and that Churchill was now Prime Minister. It was an historic moment at which to be joining the armed forces of the Crown.

★ ★ ★

Another aspect of the enigma in Leslie's character emerged in the circumstance that despite his eagerness to volunteer, he did not really enjoy the army while he was on home service. Though he venerated tradition and military ceremony, he found too many outworn attitudes that were stultifying. Perhaps, to my surprise, he felt the separation as keenly as I did, and he was homesick for me. Though outwardly gregarious, and accustomed to strict discipline at boarding school, he did not relish the coarseness and lack of privacy of life in the ranks. For my part, university became a limbo, and I lived for Leslie's letters, which he wrote with faithful regularity in all manner of noisy, public and disturbing conditions. I wrote almost daily, encouraging and assuring him of my love, and detailing the little humorous incidents that happened at home or university, and relating the gossip about those of our friends still in Edinburgh. He was particularly amused when I told him of the erratic behaviour of the lecturer I had for my special subject – the Spanish Background of English Literature. I was L.B. Walton's only pupil. It was a new course dealing with the influence on English writers of Cervantes, the Spanish mystics, and the picaresque novelists. Much of the literature he selected for analysis verged on the pornographic, and I decided that the best way to cope with the embarrassment of these solitary sessions was to affect total innocence. When he was ill, as he often was, he used to send me telegrams instead of the normal telephone message. Mr Walton lived alone in a gracious Georgian house with a monkey which was permitted to tear the wallpaper; it must have had considerable value as a companion to be excused such destructive eccentricity.

I could not now concentrate sufficiently to appreciate the distinguished quality of the staff in the English Department. The Regius Professor, John Dover Wilson, was a Shakespearean scholar of world renown, though to me he was a remote figure whose only social contact with his Honours students was a yearly invitation to his house at Balerno to partake of raw carrot sandwiches. Because I knew him so little as a man, I may have misjudged his attitude: his assumption that our first duty was to continue with our academic work, and a biased sympathy with those students who tried to defer their call-up again and again. I remember his requesting final-year students to take their examinations a term early, thus sacrificing valuable revision time, in order to accommodate one man whose further deferment was refused. Yet, sadly, Professor Dover Wilson's only son, Godfrey, a social anthropologist in South Africa, was to die there in May 1944 (as his father put it) 'as a result of the war'. This loss is referred to in Dover Wilson's autobiography *Milestones on the Dover Road* which reveals the man behind the scholar. In a letter written on 17 June 1944 (a presageful day for me), he confided his loss to Field Marshal Lord Wavell, with whom he had formed an epistolary friendship based on a common love of poetry. He also quoted Shackleton's observation that men of action whose lives are lived in hard places characteristically love poetry and beauty; this was an allusion to Wavell's anthology *Other Men's Flowers* which had been published in March of that year and which represented a selection of poems which the Field Marshal knew by heart.

In the Department, too, was Dr Arthur Melville Clark, a distinguished scholar whose lectures on Classical Background and Critical Theory were well-planned, stylish and precise; they are the only ones of which fragments still linger in my memory. Dr George Kitchin's was the stream-of-consciousness approach; he lectured almost entirely in metaphor, which illumined the subject like a lightning flash and then died away. Henry Harvey Wood, whose subject was Middle Scots literature, was later to have the distinction of being one of the founders of the Edinburgh International Festival. George Duthie lectured in his special field of Shakespearean textual criticism. I recall for his gentleness and courtesy, especially, the lecturer in English Language, Dr Odin Karel Schramm (inevitably OK Scram to the students). He had been a refugee from Belgium after the First World War, and his anguish was apparent when his country was again invaded in 1940.

Yet all this, because of my personal preoccupation with the war, I saw but through a glass darkly.

★ ★ ★

On returning to barracks after his first leave, Leslie expressed the pain of separation:

> Since Sunday there has been a dull ache inside me. When I'm separated from you I feel as if I've left a piece of myself behind. Images of you, echoes of your voice, are constantly with me. My world is split into two parts. This, the army, is my existence, but you and all the sort of world that moves round you, are my life. And I can enter into my real world quite easily from here. If I lie back at night and think – I'm with you, and you with me at once. And when I open your little book of verse – oh, how achingly sweet the vision of you seems, and I wonder why man must choose to upset his own life and make himself miserable with wars, when he could be so happy always!

Later, when he was at OCTU, he poured out similar feelings:

> I'm only existing just now. I shan't live until I come back to you. This seems strange, looking back, because I always thought I lived a full life – but I didn't until I found you; it was only a shell. You know, if it hadn't been for you, I should have been ideal material for this place – public school, university, colonial service – all crust and pretty little sense!

But you changed that, thank goodness. I think it was really because of you that I saw the best in university life, and tried to get the best out of it. The OTC was the last offering to the pukka powers . . . You've helped me to see into things; before, I really saw only the glitter. There must have been something in me. You spotted it and brought it out!

The same theme of the sadness of parting occurs again and again:

I've never felt so miserable as I did last night because of leaving you. I feel, too, that we belong entirely to each other, and it's horrible being separated from you. When I arrived back this morning, they all said, 'Got a hangover, Jock? Don't look so miserable!', so I had to get up a sort of mask, but I'm all raw underneath . . . Dearest love, I hope you weren't hurt or annoyed with me for gently sending you away from the train before it went out; but I couldn't bear the parting – I never can – especially when we weren't alone, and couldn't talk in the carriage. I hate being parted from you; and yet, I'm not the homesick kind. I've been away from home so long that I'm absolutely hardened to it . . . years of it force one to grow that skin to keep oneself from being homesick. But no child of ours will go away at eight years old if we can help it!

Leaves were anticipated with such desperate eagerness, enjoyed with taut-strung joy, and ended with anguished but stiff-lipped partings. Leslie, however, was always conscious that we were only one couple among thousands. Later, after he had received his commission, he wrote: 'I'm not the only one with an ache in his heart. I hate censoring the men's letters, because I can't help feeling it's "nosey" – and I never tell of anything I read. But I can't help saying to you, darling, that some of them miss their wives and homes very much . . . I sympathise with all my heart, though I can't say anything.' And again he commented: 'I have to censor my men's letters, and though they can't express themselves as you and I, they love just as deeply, and we're by no means unique!'

* * *

All through the summer and autumn of 1940 there was the threat of invasion. I was far from possessing Leslie's dashing courage, but I knew, with desperate stoicism, that I should be prepared to die rather than be transported to some German brothel, which we genuinely believed would be the fate of 'Aryan' types, or used as 'livestock' on some obscene stud-farm to produce children of a new master race, as we now know was actually contemplated in the perverted minds of the Nazi hierarchy.

So serious did Leslie believe the situation to be that, a half-trained gunner, he volunteered for 'Special Duties'. On 20 June he wrote me what he called a 'serious letter', the first of a spate of excited communications poured out over the following ten days. These were often written in awkward, snatched moments, and they reflect wonderfully the heightened tension gripping a young soldier of six weeks' service in the aftermath of the Bordeaux armistice and the final evacuation of the British forces from France.

> I am breaking rules by writing on this particular subject, and I don't want you to have to burn this letter, so I know you'll keep it well hidden and won't even tell your mother and father the contents.
>
> Volunteers are to be asked for to do a special job (not any more dangerous than the usual run of soldiers' risks, as far as I know) and I want to put my name down provisionally — there is a medical exam and such formalities, and one is given the chance to withdraw before beginning the job, and such things take time. So, darling, I thought I would ask you — indeed I felt I must — as we've shared everything. If you don't approve write me at once saying just 'no' in your letter, and if you do approve say 'yes'.
>
> It may mean the postponement of my commission for some time, but, darling, I don't mind that if you don't. And it will be a chance to do something at a time when action is desperately necessary, instead of this silly Army spit-and-polish nonsense. You see, dearest, I am no soldier, in the military sense, but I'd like to try my hand at it in the proper sense.

As far as I know it will be a job under the Eastern Command (that is, the Eastern *English* Command *not* abroad) and it will mean home service almost certainly, while otherwise I might be sent to Palestine or some such place. I'm afraid I can't tell you much more as I don't know any more myself, and for all I understand the thing may fizzle out.

We had Jerry over last night – five solid hours. I could hear bombs dropping, about ten miles away, I should judge, but none came near us. But he flew over our heads, masked by clouds. I expect this is going to be a regular occurrence . . .

Two days later Leslie continued his story. It seems amazing that letters like these – with their statements of military deficiencies and clear exposition of the desperate situation – were not censored, but it was all symptomatic of the country's unpreparedness, and the amateurish conduct of the war up to this time.

I'm so sorry that I can't give you any more hints on a certain subject, but no more have come my way. About seven of us have had our names accepted (provisionally). Three of the seven are POs [Potential Officers] . . . and there is always the chance that we may not be taken because we *are* cadets, but on the other hand all ranks were asked to volunteer, Officers, NCOs and men. Judging from the War Office proclamation we expect the powers that be to move swiftly, but of course we know the Army, and they probably won't, though there is, apparently, a pressing need for these volunteers.

He had appealed for my approval of his action, and I had been quite unable to restrain my anxiety; thereupon he promised to withdraw his name, but it had already gone forward, and I could not ask him to betray himself, falsely, into cowardice before his fellows. To this he now replied:

Darling, I have been feeling remorseful to say the least, ever since I wrote the last letter to you. I realise that it is pretty difficult for you to decide alone and with no advice, for none can be sought. And, dearest, as I write now, I know what your decision will be. Please believe that I didn't volunteer out of sheer bravado, or because I was seeking the bubble reputation – but principally because I felt that there was an urgent need here, and because I joined up to do something and not hunt a career, like many of my fellow POs. I know that's a spiteful remark, and perhaps I shouldn't have made it, but I've been just a little soured by some of my fellow cadets . . . I'm very anxious to hear your views on my doings. I do hope, and I'm pretty sure you'll understand, that there is no adventure-seeking in my action. But I consider that we are in very serious danger of invasion, and that's why I volunteered, because I suspect that this job would be connected with the repulse of an expected attack – so the army ought to move quickly. If the other chaps like to 'fiddle' at such a time they jolly well can, but I won't. Please don't think me a Blimp, dear thing!

The letter of 25 June, with all its amazing candour, came with this apology:

I am writing this during a spell of guard duty, with one eye on the look-out, so it may be a bit jerky . . .

I propose to give you some information which will surprise you, and which I know you will keep to yourself.

Since the crisis in France, even before the Armistice, there has been to all intents and purposes no Royal Artillery. If we are to be a beleaguered fortress, then only AA and heavy coastal guns are needed. As you know, I am 'on active service'. Well, I can assure you that's no catchword. We are stationed on an aerodrome near Harrogate – at least not very far away – and our job is both to guard it and to prepare for an invasion by parachute troops. Every night there is a series of 'stands-to' . . . We carry ball ammunition, and for weeks since leaving Harrogate have done no artillery drill, being neither AA nor heavy. Instead I am being rapidly trained to be an infantry soldier, as far as I can see, for we do a great deal of rifle work, and machine-gun, too. Jerry has been over several times lately, and we expect to be bombed any night. We don't go to shelters, but prepare to resist with rifles and Lewis guns. If my safety in connection with the new job is bothering you, then I assure you there isn't a night here which mightn't be my last – we thought we were for it a few nights ago. There are new and secret factories being built here, and Jerry knows all about them.

The new job I don't know about myself. But the requirements are: swimming of a reasonable standard; A1 fitness; 'good heart' both physically and mentally; immunity as far as possible to seasickness; 'resolute will', as the army puts it. One of our NCOs, a pretty shrewd fellow, deduces that it will be coastal patrol work in motor boats with the object of dealing with enemy troops landing in those little rubber dinghies used by German air troop-carriers. I think his suggestion is very probable, and as we are in very grave danger of invasion it's obviously the place where we are needed most, especially when one thinks that artillery is being transformed (at least a good deal of it is) . . .

Darling, I'm not trying to make your flesh creep, but by my reckoning a secret place like this isn't safe, and the new job is *home* at least, as some troops may go East. The long gunnery training I could have stuck, but this is more vital. Nobody wants artillery officers now: there are plenty to go on with . . .

On 26 June Leslie had some definite news for me, conveyed in an excited and somewhat disjointed letter which in the light of events much later in his army career has extraordinary irony:

The volunteers were all interviewed today and told that the job had been divided into two parts: 1. Parachutists and 2. Still vague, but probably coast work, as I thought. They want men badly for the first, but I refused point-blank as it means absolute certain death. I think only one man has so far volunteered for this, and I am told that his wife died recently and that he doesn't care about things now. My darling, you can rest assured that the only time I would ever go for that first choice would be if something happened to you. I shouldn't care about things then either. But I couldn't deliberately do a foolhardy thing like that even if my life depended on it. It's the first time I've heard of the formation of a British Parachutist Corps; and when one reads how we are going to murder the enemy on the same job it puts one off. It's much too like the Glorious Twelfth for my liking!

Indeed this was the absolute beginning of a parachute formation in the British Army. Even before the armistice in France, Churchill was considering 'butcher and bolt' raids on enemy-held territory, and on 22 June 1940 he issued a directive to the Joint Chiefs of Staff to the effect that, 'We ought to have a corps of at least 5,000 parachute troops'. A mere four days later Leslie wrote to me of these momentous developments; and in his letter of 26 June he made clear his willingness to take all risks except that of jumping out of aeroplanes:

I have still left my name down for number 2, but it can be removed any time up to the medical examination . . . I honestly want your definite approval or I will withdraw my name, and I mean that. I have weighed it up, and consider that it is no more risky than the job I'm doing now (as I've said before) and far more important and necessary – well, I shouldn't say 'important' or you'll think I'm glory-hunting, but it certainly is a vital job, in the sense that it's got to be done quickly and willingly. As I read your letter, I could almost sense your thoughts: 'He's going to do it anyway, whether I like it or not . . .', and I couldn't bear that, for I've never looked at it that way. I won't plead for your approval – give it to me freely, dear thing, or not at all . . .

Since I've been 'on active service', I've learned more than in all my dreary days at Harrogate. The life has been much less 'army', and we have learned to handle small arms quite well, which is what is required for this new job . . . Please trust me. I wouldn't go rushing into a suicide squad: how could I when I have you? But I do so want to do something really useful, and

I think I can handle this better than artillery stuff. Am I defaulting, do you think? . . . Since I've been here doing infantry stuff I've enjoyed it as far as one can enjoy the army, and I'll never sneer at the PBI again. But nevertheless I intend to persevere with the artillery unless something unexpected turns up. We are very carefully watched, and budding infantry officers or men are quickly weeded out and transferred whether they like it or not, if the artillery thinks that they show 'infantry' aptitude, and honestly, I don't think that the one is more hazardous than the other. I believe that the whole of the armed forces are in the same mess, and that the civil population is not far behind either . . . We're all in the soup now, and a full-scale onslaught is coming shortly. That's why I wanted to do something quickly before Hitler had got into his proper swing for this new attack . . . Dearest, don't worry about anything concerning me. I'll keep my promise. It will take more than a war to snuff either of us out. We'll both see that 2000 AD yet!

As it turned out, however, he was not called upon to fulfil his commitment as a volunteer for Special Duties, though in September, when he was at OCTU, he came very near to action in this country. From the information in the following letter written on 10 September (once again, it seems, amazingly uncensored), it appeared that the Germans were thought to have effected a small landing:

You will have seen in the papers [Leslie wrote, in an excited note, uncharacteristically disregarding grammar and syntax] that the bells rang out on Sunday. [This was the signal for invasion.] Well, there was a small invasion, in spite of the papers' denial. I know this because I was aide-de-camp to an officer, and got 'all the news', and saw the telegram announcing that all had been caught. Most came by air and landed, but some tried to land from the sea, but I don't think they did. Anyhow, we heard rumours on Saturday night, and on Sunday we 'stood to' for hours. We were ordered to prepare for active service, and were ready to leave at half an hour's notice for anywhere, with 48 hours' rations. They let us go for lunch – I wrote to you – and then they took us back, but everything was safely over by tea, and the telegram saying so came about then. But we all thought for a while we were 'for it'. I was quite worried myself when I wrote. [Then he added – the enigma of his attitude to war and danger manifesting itself again –] You must never think that I look upon this as an adventure, because I don't, though, to be frank, I came pretty near to it in September '39!

The truth about this 'invasion' did not fully emerge until a statement was made by Clement Attlee in the House of Commons on 18 November 1946. During the first week of September 1940, flotillas of barges and transports were spotted making for the ports and river estuaries of Holland, Belgium and northern France. Then on the night of 7 September the Admiralty signalled the Home Fleet to action stations, and units of the army were ordered to stand to. Also on 7 September, the more serious directive 'Cromwell' was issued. That was the No. 1 alert – invasion to be expected within twelve hours – and all troops were to be at battle stations. That night 300 German bombers, escorted by twice as many fighters, dropped high explosive and incendiary bombs on the London docks. The 'Cromwell' signal had been sent only to Eastern and Southern Commands, and to HQ London District; but rumour and excitement spread throughout the country. In Northern, Western and Scottish Commands not all staff officers (at this time often young and inexperienced) knew what 'Cromwell' meant; some thought it was simply an alert; others that the invasion had actually begun.

★ ★ ★

In August 1940, after his three months in the ranks, Leslie was sent to the Royal Artillery OCTU at Ilkley. Here, naturally, he found the company more congenial, but he had difficulty in wrestling with the mathematics necessary for mastering the science of gunnery. He should never have been in the artillery at all – neither from mathematical ability nor temperament – but at university the Battery had been considered the 'better' unit. The cadets were expected to attain in six months the standards reached by regular officers in peacetime on a much longer course in a chosen career. Also, the psychological pressure of being continually watched and assessed for one's suitability as an officer, and the constant fear of failure and return to the ranks, deflated Leslie's natural buoyancy. His slight childhood stammer (acquired from being forced to be right-handed when his natural inclination was otherwise) returned, and he was sent to the unit psychiatrist. 'He didn't ask me,' said Leslie, 'which school did I go to – was it Eton or merely Marlborough – which caused me to view him with immense respect!' The psychiatrist was reassuring. Leslie did not have the personality of the typical stammerer, and the disability would disappear when he left OCTU; as indeed it did.

Meanwhile, he sought comfort in letters to me:

> I'm up to the eyes in work for the first time in my life. Today we were turned out for a practice emergency at five this morning, so we've had a mere fourteen-hour day. To make matters worse, I'll *have* to do extra work in the evening, as there's a colossal amount to be learned – it's truly appalling. We have to know the whole of the organisation of the *whole* army in the first month, for one thing . . . the fact that grates me most is that I haven't time to read your books – I haven't opened one since I came here . . . I've taken up my fencing again. There is a Major Dobrée here, who in civil life is the English Prof. at Leeds. I didn't know that until I heard him lecture, and then I knew by his highly entertaining manner that he wasn't a 'military man', although he looks very dapper – silver hair and moustache. He runs the fencing.

In this appraisal, as it turned out, Leslie was both right and wrong. Bonamy Dobrée had been a regular field gunner before the First World War, had resigned his commission, gone to Cambridge (where he gained a Fencing Blue), and had only thereafter become an academic of considerable distinction. In 1939 he had renounced the world of Restoration and Augustan literature for the Royal Artillery once again.

This OCTU [Leslie went on] is getting more and more like a public school cum kindergarten. Now the latest thing is that our troop lacks the 'team spirit', and games are compulsory from now on. I have my fencing, so that's all right . . . As for 'team spirit', I've been brought up on that all my life and it makes me scream . . . Bless you, darling – if I hadn't you, I really would give up [trying for a commission]. I keep asking myself, 'Is it worth it?', but I think it is, even if only to get this war finished a day sooner, or keep some poor devils from killing themselves . . . If it weren't for you, I would feel that life wasn't worth living, but because of you, I feel that it is worth living, and living *well*, and I'll do my best . . . I look ahead to the time when the war is over, and we can be together for always, and this existence seems like a dream that will pass in a flash. And then I think back on all the happy times we had until the war affected our lives, and this keeps the present away from me. Sometimes, when I remember how you used to hurry (going clip-clop in your wooden shoes) across the Quad or out of Minto House and come smiling to meet me standing with affected nonchalance on the street or under the arches – I feel that I could just cry like a baby. Yes, you may be surprised at that, but it's true. And when I think of how I hurt you because I fretted about getting into the war, it makes me feel a swine. Please forgive me. I didn't mean it, although that's a poor excuse. Nothing in the world matters to me really except you. As long as we have each other, we can make or find beauty in our lives. I'm more convinced than ever that the most important thing is human relationships. Catastrophes like this one never did or will do anybody any good.

The enigma was apparent in this same letter. I think the explanation is that, like any humane person who had much to live for, Leslie had dreaded war; but war had come, and youth and idealism and excitement had taken over. But now, at this time, he felt he was not *in* the war and had merely lost the happiness of peace. Despite such moments of despondency, which vanished when he went into action,

Leslie never regretted volunteering, nor ceased to believe in the cause for which he was prepared to fight. But 'fight' was the operative word; he was impatient of what he saw as a time-wasting kind of training. He railed at the army's 'ponderous inefficiency' and expressed regret at the news in June 1941 that Wavell was to be relieved of his Middle East command. 'He was a live wire in a dull army,' Leslie commented, 'quite unorthodox, which shocked his fellow top brass, but I expect he'll be a Field Marshal yet.' Leslie would have been the first to share my amusement at the impression he created: a very junior officer prepared to promote a general! Even as a raw cadet with a white band on his forage cap and white tabs on his epaulettes he had had decided opinions about the workings of the army, and the conduct of the war. But there was substance in his admiration of Wavell, and justice in his criticism of the army's complacency.

Leslie himself did not really fit into a regular unit. I do not mean that he was rebellious against necessary discipline, and certainly not resentful of hardship and discomfort. He was popular with his fellow cadets and, when commissioned, with his men; and though he maintained strict standards for himself, was tolerant of others. But the outdated organisation and 'heartless bureaucracy' of the machine irked him. On foreign service, however, and more particularly in a special unit where the rules were more practical and the ideas less conventional, he was as happy as the context of war allowed.

Of course Leslie was not the only young soldier to feel this way. The poet Alun Lewis spoke about being 'crucified by repression, regimentation, procedures, and the taboos of hierarchy', and of how his attempts to humanise the army by means of debating societies and current affairs courses met with resentment and hostility. And there is, more cynically, that well-known poem 'Naming of Parts', written by Henry Reed, who was later released from the army to work at Bletchley Park. In answer to my attempts to soothe and encourage, Leslie replied:

> Darling, I think you could make a good soldier out of almost any man . . . and I mean that nicely, for I should like to be a good soldier myself. But that's quite distinct from the stupid militarism that exists in the service, and yet this army is freer

of it than many European armies. I really admire a *good* soldier — even though he may be a regular — but he is a very rare bird and one meets him so seldom, although I rather think our troop officer comes near the mark. I think that a real soldier would do anything for his men, but not torment them as we're tormented. And I'll jolly well remember that if I get my commission.

But OCTU had its lighter moments. Leslie wrote describing one exercise:

The first position we occupied today was just off the road in a grassy field. The Colonel was there, and when a man with a cart full of turnips came along and shouted at him, everybody sat up. It was apparently the man's land we were on, and he said loudly to the Colonel, 'Hey, you, come here!' The Old Man turned livid and screamed, 'How dare you talk to me like that!', absolutely shaking with rage. We were shaking with laughter. It was worth all the weary days spent here to see the old humbug, at whose gaze we should tremble, being told off by a ploughman. High words followed, and then the man rode off swearing. The Colonel bolted off home, too, swearing. And in the next field we went into they turned a bull on us.

All this time Leslie's conscience smote him that he was still in training; this in part accounted for his disillusion.

I feel it wrong, somehow, that all we lads here should be living in an absolute backwater. The war here is just a news- and wireless-story, and for some a memory of France and Norway. I've actually been dipping into a military work for pleasure. It's a Penguin called *New Ways of War* by Tom Wintringham, professional soldier and now a captain in the army. [Wintringham had been in the RFC and RAF in the First World War and had in 1937 commanded the British battalion of the International Brigade in the Spanish Civil

War.] The War Office nearly had a fit when this book came out, and wouldn't listen to him until the invasion scare grew serious. He exposes the ridiculous tactics of the army, its old-fashioned, rigid conservatism, that won't grasp the new facts thrust under its nose. The book interested me quite a bit, and it's mostly true, and not heavy-going. If you could bear to look through it, you might get some idea of the army and what I'm up against – but don't say you will, just to please me.

This book was to have a lasting effect on Leslie's thinking, on his subsequent army career and, indeed, on his destiny.

I did try to take an interest in Leslie's 'work', and he appreciated this.

It makes it so much easier for me knowing that you're always behind me, encouraging and approving. I mean, I'm glad you don't hate the sight of me in khaki. I don't like it much myself, because I know it doesn't stand altogether for all the nice things the press say; but I have to wear it, and I'm so pleased that you can tolerate it!

He was very sensitive to my feeling about not being able to share his world, and he often wore 'civvies' on leave, even though it exposed him to the slur of being non-combatant. I had mentioned that one of my lecturers – a delicate man – was about to be called up. Leslie commiserated:

He'll hate the army, possibly in a different way from the way I do – especially the ranks. When he gets to an OCTU he'll perk up, because he'll leave all the squalid brutality behind. You helped me to shut that out; let's hope that he can. A fellow like him said that this place [OCTU] was bearable because it had a faint atmosphere of scholarship (he was a physicist). So it has, if you're a BSc; but I'm living in an Inferno of logs, sines and horrid barometric demons. I really see, although I don't approve, why RA officers consider themselves 'one above' the Infantry. They fairly have to sweat mentally to get there. I'm very lucky – shortly after the war began, new POs for the Artillery had to have university standard of maths, not just school certificate. But, once you're in, you're in, so I'm all right – so far!

Leslie's mood began to darken. It seemed, he wrote, 'that all the greatest happiness in the world has its roots in pain . . . I think, somehow, that you know that better than I do, my darling. And yet, if it were not bound up with pain, would, indeed, human love be so great and so prized? Oh, I'm so glad we have our love to hold fast to in this rotten and crumbling world. I can't help feeling, especially after the Coventry raid and its reprisals, that the world *we* know is either rotten or crumbling; and I prefer to think the latter, because we can always try to build a new one . . . I'm sorry, but all the wretchedness of this war boils over in me sometimes . . .' In November he wrote: 'I bought a Flanders poppy today with mixed feelings. Don't you think that they might leave out the verse about "If ye break faith . . .", because isn't that just what we've done? The public puts the wrong interpretation on that verse, I'm sure.'

Yet, in spite of disillusion and frustration, privations and partings, boredom, bombings and the blackout, there was a champagne atmosphere – a brittleness, if you like – about the war. Emotions were heightened and sharpened, every moment of happiness savoured – who knew but that it might be the last? There was a peculiar poignancy and depth – perhaps *value* in love that could not be consummated, and which was always under threat. There was also the consciousness that we were all taking part in a great enterprise, something bigger than ourselves. Youth had a purpose – even if were only to put an end to that purpose. We lived for 'after the war', and looked no further, and were therefore spared the sense of futility that often assails the youth of today. *The Times* fourth leader of 3 July 1940 diagnosed the cause of this mood that was euphoric against all the odds: 'We have almost ceased to look forward . . . holidays, peace, victory are no longer on the agenda . . . the days of looking forward used to pass so slowly and heavily because they had merely to be lived through for the sake of others to come, but now the days are all lived for their own sake.'

As a city, Edinburgh escaped very lightly from German bombing. My parents and I lived in a flat, and the lady on the ground floor had one of her rooms made gas-proof, and all the neighbours congregated there when the sirens sounded. On the nights of 13 and 14 February 1941 there were heavy raids on Clydebank. We sat up all night, recklessly drinking our week's tea ration, listening to the planes droning overhead and being shamefully relieved when they passed on to somewhere else – we did not know where, though we could guess. Our own anti-aircraft fire, though of dubious effectiveness, gave us considerable comfort. The situation seemed quite unreal, and I was surprised to find that I was not at all terrified – perhaps because I knew that there was absolutely nothing I could do if a bomb had my name on it. This realisation ought to have helped me to understand Leslie's attitude to risk-taking for a cause; but it did not. It taught me only that it may be easier to face danger oneself than to imagine someone one loves facing it.

By February the Officer Training course was nearing its end, and Leslie expressed his fears for the final exam: 'This is the calm before the storm. The exam begins at 9.30 and they've given us an hour before it to ourselves to revise. But I'm in such a fizz that I couldn't work, so I'm beginning a letter to you to calm me down. Exams here are horrible. I don't think I ever fizzed so much at University, though I remember your walking me round the mummy section [the Egyptian Gallery of the Royal Scottish Museum] in Chambers Street once.'

* * *

Leslie 'passed out' successfully, and having been commissioned into the Royal Artillery, was posted to a smart Scottish regiment, the Ayrshire Yeomanry (Earl of Carrick's Own). Scotland's senior Yeomanry regiment had been mobilised in September 1939 as a cavalry unit: the officers had brought their own hunters into the regiment, and training had been anachronistic sword-drill. At the end of that year the Ayrshire Yeomanry was told that it must convert into an artillery unit. Given the choice of becoming a Field, Medium or Anti-Tank regiment, the mess had opted to be field-gunners, solely on account of the appeal of the word 'Field'. Naturally the cavalry of the line, and equally the volunteer Yeomanry regiments, had been sad to lose their horses. As a versifier among them expressed it:

> No more, alas, the head-tossed foam, the fretful foot that pawed:
> Oh glory that was Tetrarch's might, oh drabness that is Ford!

In compensation, the commanding officer of the Ayrshire Yeomanry ordered a yellow horseshoe to be painted on the door of every vehicle.

Not very enthusiastic attention had been paid to gunnery instruction, and amateurish attendance at courses had been punctuated by beagling and fox-hunting. Some months later the Ayrshire Yeomanry was divided into two regiments: as 151 and 152 Field Regiments, RA, they were to serve with distinction as parts of armoured divisions – the former landing in Normandy in June 1944 and fighting through Belgium, Holland and Germany to the Elbe; and the latter in North Africa, Italy and Austria. However reluctant the yeomen may initially have been to become gunners, their record of achievement in their new role was a total vindication. Leslie was posted to 152 Field Regiment (Ayrshire Yeomanry).

★ ★ ★

On the strength of his commission, we became engaged. It was only a prestige strength, because Leslie had to ask the jeweller to reserve the ring (it cost £30) for a month until he could pay for it. Young officers who had only their pay were perpetually hard-up. There were expensive uniforms to buy; some of the kit – such as riding-boots and breeches for an artillery regiment nevertheless anxious to keep as much of its county cavalry style as it could – seemed quite ridiculous in wartime and, incidentally, when Leslie went on a course to the artillery training camp at Larkhill on Salisbury Plain, he reported that he had had the life teased out of him on account of this uniform. Someone actually thought he was Polish, for the combination of the rather old-fashioned kit with the silver-and-gold winged griffon cap- and collar-badges had a certain Central-European look. There are letters mentioning difficulties over small sums, which would seem ludicrous even to unemployed youngsters today; and once Leslie affirmed jubilantly: 'We've got two weeks' full pay, having missed some at Harrogate, and so I got 28 shillings [£1.40]. I feel uproariously rich!' When he was posted to the far north of Scotland, and was due to come home on leave, he explained: 'I'll be paying my own rail-fare this time, and it's quite hefty. I could have wangled a third travel warrant (only two allowed per year) and trusted Records not to notice it, but I'm cursed (or blessed) with a conscience. Because the poor gunners have to pay their fares I reckon I can pay mine, too, don't you? I don't care two hoots about diddling the government, but I just can't take advantage over the men, even though I *did* lose my warrant last financial year.' Then he added, on an inconsequent, uncommercial note: 'I feel there is something imperishable and sacred between us . . . somehow your sweetness and loveliness makes me feel there is a God to take care of us both . . . I can never imagine any kind of life without you . . .'

CHAPTER 4

The difficult tolerance of all that is
Mere rigid brute routine.
ALUN LEWIS: 'AFTER DUNKIRK'

We were engaged, but there was absolutely no prospect of marriage.

Ferryden, near Montrose, was Leslie's first posting, in March 1941. His billet was a cottage shared with another officer, a captain of uncertain temper, which made the domesticity less cosy. (They later became good friends.) Their troop of the 152 Field Regiment (Ayrshire Yeomanry) was attached to a unit of the Polish Army stationed nearby, and together their function was coastal defence. The Yeomanry's ordnance at Montrose consisted of two antiquated cannon from Edinburgh Castle. A Polish colonel, Leslie reported, 'a very nice fellow, terribly polite', brought his men 'to get some practice drill on our "Old Mortality", so we've had to polish it – no pun intended'. A very drunk naval officer whom Leslie and his troop commander met one night in a Montrose hotel insisted, and kept on insisting, that they were Polish – the cap-badge again. Captain Ellis countered by asking him in return if he was the cloakroom attendant.

As the threat of invasion had receded, coastal defence could not have seemed an occupation of first priority. However, there were compensations. Leslie's mother had an old friend in Montrose, and she invited me to stay for a weekend; also the town was within reach of Edinburgh for a 'forty-eight-hour' leave. But after a few weeks there was a disconcerting rumour: 'I feel so much in need of you tonight,' Leslie confessed. 'I don't know what it is, but all day I've been missing you, more than usual . . . Oh, I love you, my dearest, dearest girl, and I'm so afraid we're going to move shortly . . . life seems so terribly mundane in the army; it's always a question of one's arranging the next day's food or sending in a frantic hurry for more toilet-paper because it's run out and the lads are choking the drains with newspaper.' And then there crept in a wistful note: 'I find myself missing "history" . . . I wish I were back listening to old VHG [Vivian Hunter Galbraith, Professor of History at Edinburgh], making wisecracks about Willy I's mother, and discovering that somebody had 10 pigs on his manor . . . I might have been rewarded by Clio for worshipping her instead of trying to alter her complexion.'

The rumour was indeed true, and the little Montrose detachment joined the whole regiment in Caithness. Travel from there was difficult for Leslie, and impossible for me. (It was a restricted zone.) We were fortunate that during his posting in the north he was chosen to attend a messing officers' course at the Lowland Division depot at Glencorse just outside Edinburgh. Although the subtleties of the cellar and the niceties of the different cuts of meat seemed concerns of peacetime, and odd priorities when the regiment's assorted guns had all too little ammunition for comfort, we accepted the boon of time together which the Ayrshire Yeomanry's gastronomic demands afforded us. On his return to Wick he reported that he had received a telephone call from RHQ informing him that he had been appointed 'Messing Officer, Canteen Officer and Education Officer – Pooh Bah'.

There was at times a certain friction between the Yeomanry officers and the gunner officers who had been posted to the regiment since the outbreak of war, and whom the original cavalry element considered interlopers. Leslie expressed the incomers' point of view:

> The Mess is often boring. When the gunner subalterns are together, talk is quite cheery, because we have a playwright, a university student and a budding CA. But when the yeomen roll in, it's nothing but huntin' . . . We have a padre now, shared with another outfit. He is C. of E. and doesn't wear a dog-collar but an ordinary collar and tie, with the result that people think he's a Rifle Brigade officer. He is a good fellow, a cousin of Walford Davis, and a pleasant change from the huntin' yeomen. Needless to say, they don't know how to handle him.

The Caithness landscape was barren and treeless, and the area remote; in United Kingdom terms it was like being banished to Siberia. But gradually the bleak countryside exerted its own strange fascination, as Leslie expressed it to me: 'Last night I saw the most beautiful sunset I've seen in Caithness – or ever, I think. Oh, love, I wished you'd been there. I was on a hilltop and Halkirk lay beneath me, and it looked like the Celestial City, all wreathed in violet mist, and the hills to the south were deep purple with a sky like an artist's palette behind – oh, if only I could paint! Dearest love, it was like the end of *The Pilgrim's Progress*, and it filled my heart with you.' Perhaps in this lonely, treeless land, skies were noticeable as the one variable beauty; certainly Leslie seemed particularly aware of sunsets: 'It was such a lovely sky, and I seemed to be looking right into the eye of heaven. Somehow it gave me a tightness round my heart, and I wanted you here with me, more than I can say.'

Where the regiment was stationed the local 'big house' was Stirkoke, residence of Kate, Lady Horne, widow of General Lord Horne. Lady Horne showed generous hospitality to the local troops. There was a regular Sunday tea-party for the officers of the Yeomanry, and she gave them the run of her library, of which Leslie made good use. There was something rather touching about the aged widow of the late Master Gunner of St James's Park taking under her wing these very young artillery subalterns. Her husband had been commissioned from Woolwich more than sixty years before, and she had no son. Leslie wrote thus about Stirkoke and its owner:

> Tomorrow we have a spit-and-polish church parade, and then in the afternoon our weekly tea with old Lady Horne – she really is exactly like Cicily Courtneige as the colonel's daughter; but all the same, she keeps a very nice plum cake. The cook (one of five) has promised to make some for us if she can get the stuff . . . You would find this an amazing house. It is hung with trophies of war, flags, uniforms, medals, portraits, and citations of honour. Autographed photographs of royalty and famous statesmen sit beside mementos of some of the most renowned soldiers of the century. This house lives completely in the past – not

surprising, considering the age of its owner. It marks the end
of a long line of soldiers – a military dynasty is something
new to me. It's a little depressing, and in peacetime would be
awful, but somehow it fits in with the spirit of the times . . .
Lord Horne's study is lined with military memoirs. I've had
a look at some of the campaign histories, and truly every one
had its pages uncut: apparently even Generals are not above
a little eyewash.

On one of those Sundays, when some of the 'County' were present,
Lady Horne thought to ask about the plumbing alterations in progress
at the Ayrshire Yeomanry camp. 'How's your water?' she bellowed at
one of the officers, quite oblivious of the double entendre.

It was all very like peacetime soldiering, with plenty of
opportunity for the diversions beloved of the Yeomanry. As a public
schoolboy in the Perthshire countryside, Leslie had grown up
accustomed to outdoor pursuits and bloodsports; but when I had
expressed a horror of shooting wildlife, he gave up this practice. Now
he avoided it whenever possible, and I realised it must not have been
easy for him to be 'different' in his regiment. He never complained,
however, and there was no reproach in his relating that 'most of the
Mess is out at a dance; the rest of them are hunting rabbit with Mills
bombs; so I've settled down with the *Essays* of Montaigne and a right
good programme of Mozart – from a German station . . . Then they
brought me in your parcel and the half-formed thoughts in my head
insisted that they be sent to you. Darling, I like the Stevenson [a
leather-bound copy of the poems of RLS]: it has a nice, well-worn
appearance. I'm like you – I love old things with good lines.' Then he
went on: 'We live a quiet, domestic sort of life up here. At tea-time we
make toast, and at night a bed-time cup of cocoa. The Colonel thinks
this should be a rest-camp for officers who have seen too much of the
de Guise and the Havana . . .' Apparently, when the regiment had been
stationed in Edinburgh, they had divided their evenings between
these two smart 'night spots'.

Leslie found some of his duties ludicrous in the extreme:
'Tomorrow I'm going to sit solemnly as a member of a court of
enquiry into the disposal and casting of clothes; so you can picture

three grave figures – a captain and two subalterns – deciding with much profound thought if the pair of underpants before their consideration is fit to be worn, or should it be renewed.'

There was boredom, too, of life in Caithness, so remote in place and purpose from the spirit in which Leslie had volunteered. He depended a great deal on listening to music, and once commented that 'our wireless is defunct, and has been sent for a rest cure, and so I've no waltzes to beguile the hours, only the mazurka of a motorcycle . . . [He had to learn to ride one, and had become rather fond of it.] Your love is a tower of strength and bears me up over all this horrid war – nonetheless horrid though it is peaceful for me.' There was a warning sign here which I chose to ignore. One of the reasons why Leslie was not really happy in the army at this time was his feeling of shame that he was doing so little, and that he was in a remote and safe place – but, *I* was glad!

In November 1941, 152 Field Regiment (Ayrshire Yeomanry) made the long trek from Caithness to Epping in Essex. This was quite an operation, involving as it did the movement of 700 men, 150 trucks and other vehicles and, of course, the guns, over the still rather primitive road network of pre-war Scotland and England. The journey took more than a week. Leslie managed to write to me every evening. At the end of the second day he described how he had been patrol officer in the RHQ convoy on the road north of Carrbridge on Speyside, riding up and down the column on his motorbike 'like a sheepdog with lambs', and watching over broken-down vehicles including even their own Light Aid Detachment. In that one day he covered 300 miles on his bike. From Dumfries he explained some of the conditions of the trek: 'Today I had to leave Perth early and buzz on ahead to Carstairs to arrange for a petrol issue to the regiment. I passed through Stirling, and stopped to cash a much-needed cheque. This move is rather expensive, for no billeting arrangements are made for officers – we are expected to fix our own accommodation in hotels . . .'

The physical conditions of the new camp at Epping were far more 'civilised', and the officers could get easily to London; but the enigma in Leslie's character surfaced again with the guilty feeling that things *were* better: he had not joined the army to have tea in Fortnum's, or to dine at the Junior Carlton, of which one of his friends in the Yeomanry was a member. At this time he was attached to RHQ, and the frustration of so many administrative – almost civilian – duties clearly irked him. His letters mention such un-military matters as 'shopping expeditions' to Piccadilly on behalf of the Mess. On one occasion he reported accompanying the adjutant to buy an overcoat – a British Warm: 'We've all got them now – mine is still beautiful, and the only one with a bustle!' In spite of his dislike of the trifling tedium of inactive soldiering, he still retained his endearing little vanities about uniforms.

Moreover, the regiment ceased to be a happy one. A popular commanding officer, Reggie Houldsworth, was replaced by a new colonel who rapidly set himself at odds with the Mess. Not least of his offences was his ordering of the regiment to remove its ancient and traditional collar badges and buttons, and to replace them with the grenade badges and regular buttons of the Royal Artillery. All were weary of being moved about from one end of the country to the other, and some officers chafed at hearing of their friends in other units going overseas. Leslie certainly felt they were forgotten, and resented what he saw as their idleness. I think that this malaise was widespread among soldiers serving at home. The navy had, traditionally, been pre-eminent – 'The navy's here!' was the great cry of confidence – and now the new glamour-boys were the RAF. The army, until the successes in the Desert War, were just 'the Brown Jobs', and 'browned off' was the expression most often on the soldiers' lips. The navy and the RAF were constantly in action, but at this time in the war the army did not have a very colourful role.

By the early months of 1942 a mood of deep pessimism had set in: 'Darling,' Leslie wrote, 'I'm worried just now; I think there's something wrong with this nation. Do you remember the story of the Roman senator who, when Rome was at her zenith, sighed for the old days when she was only a city state, but had other purposes besides luxury? I think that cap just about fits.' I imagine that the only luxury he could have been envisaging then was preoccupation with food and drink in the Mess. Some officers did run up bills far beyond their means. Certainly, though Leslie loved beautiful things, he feared materialism and its overtaking the more important issues of life. Later, in North Africa, he was to have similar misgivings about idleness.

In another letter he remarked: 'I read a speech by the Archbishop of York the other day, saying that we mustn't hate the Germans. What do you think? It seems to me that one can't go to war successfully unless one *does* hate a bit. And as for this separation of Nazis and Germans, it doesn't work. They're all tarred with the same brush anyway. I once thought I could never hate anybody, but I find myself getting pretty near to it nowadays – not least out of personal spite because my own life has been so pulled about – and yours, too.' He had been reading Dame Laura Knight's autobiography, and commented, with a note of bitterness that was new: 'It makes me more than ever envious of people who wield the brush or chisel. The only thing I can wield is a rifle. Nice commentary on modern civilisation – educated for 20 years and turned out as a professional killer!'

Indeed, both Leslie and I were now tired and strained to the limit. We had known and loved one another for four and a half years, two and a half in wartime, and the prospect of our getting married or the war ending seemed as remote as ever. It was also a low ebb in the nation's fortunes. Conscription for women had been introduced on 31 December 1941. I was within six months of my final examinations, and it was accepted that in those circumstances women should finish their degrees; but, nevertheless, I felt restless and guilty. When Leslie came home on leave in January, he was withdrawn and morose. I had never before seen him like this. In 1940, and again in 1941, he lost cousins, the elder of whom had been like a big brother to him at school. Freddie Fairweather had been killed in a flying accident after surviving the Battle of Britain, and his younger brother Kenneth had given in to his mother's entreaties not to join the RAF; but 'there is no armour against fate', and he had lost his life serving with the army in the Western Desert. Now we had word that yet another cousin – a South African, Ernest Gardner – had been killed at Sidi Rizegh, and his brother taken prisoner. Ernest had come to Britain on holiday with his parents in 1938 and had stayed on to attend the Edinburgh College of Art. During the summer vacation of 1939 he went home to Johannesburg, and on the outbreak of war joined up in the Transvaal Scottish. This latest death hit Leslie hard. 'Three cousins now,' he lamented, 'and we were all such friends!'

I felt I could not reach him, and in my own overstrung state was not able to be still and wait for the black mood to pass – perhaps because I feared it would not pass, since it had an even deeper cause than these bereavements. I knew Leslie wanted to have a chance to hit back; and he had not joined the army to be one of the 'gentlemen of England now abed'. I realised that it was for my sake that he was taking no steps towards making his part in the war more active; and yet I *could* not speak out and give him my blessing to leave his regiment and volunteer for service overseas. It was a wretched leave. And when he returned to barracks his letters seemed short and factual. I could not bear the situation, and so I committed the unbelievable, the ultimate folly – I wrote a letter breaking off our engagement. Leslie replied by saying he was completely stunned. In his dispirited state he did not fight back, saying only, that to please me perhaps he had been trying to be what he could not be, and that he was really a little 'wilder' than I had realised. He asked if I would come to London to talk things over. I refused. 'So, "Come, let us kiss and part",' he said. 'I shall certainly go abroad.' He expressed gratitude for all the happiness I had given him and wished me well. This wrung my heart but, in my preoccupation with my own feelings, I did not perceive the pain behind the stiff words. I cannot now imagine why I did not have the generosity and courage to let him go. Anything would have been better than being thus estranged.

'Si la jeunesse savait . . .'

CHAPTER 5

But had I wist before I kiss'd
    That love had been sae ill to win,
I'd lock'd my heart in a case of gold
And pinn'd it with a siller pin.
                                'WALY, WALY'

I was indeed broken-hearted in the manner of the old Scots ballads, especially as I felt I had been the more to blame. I realised that I had indeed tried, for my own comfort, to make of Leslie a tamer image. I now shut myself away with my books, too long neglected, and somehow managed to get a good degree. I think that my misery, and the fact that I was sitting my finals during the fall of Tobruk, minimised the importance of the examinations and, accordingly, my nervous anxiety over them.

Though I expected never to see Leslie again, his influence yet continued strong. I felt guilty that I had done so little for the war effort. Certainly I had worked in a servicemen's canteen, and registered as being available at a first-aid post in the event of a blitz on Edinburgh. There was also compulsory fire-watching at the university: this was hazardous in the blackout on account of the cupolas, skylights and hatches, and the general unevenness of the roofs of the Old Quad.

However, now that I had graduated, I decided that I could not remain at home in a reserved occupation such as teaching. My fearfulness had been the flaw in my relationship with Leslie. Though too late, I felt I must atone for my lack of courage and understanding. Therefore I applied to the Women's Royal Naval Service; but they were not recruiting at the time. This was by far the most favoured of the women's services, and gave priority to those with naval connections. I had had an uncle, killed when his ship was torpedoed in the First World War, who, as a midshipman, had sailed round Cape Horn on a windjammer. As I did not even get an interview with the WRNS, I had no chance to boast of this remotest of qualifications. So I then wrote to the Civil Service Commissioners, asking if there were vacancies in any of the ministries directly concerned with the war.

Meanwhile, I took a temporary job in charge of the Medical Reading Room, which for the duration of the war was housed in the Anatomy Museum of the University of Edinburgh Medical School. The rows of foetal monstrosities preserved in formaldehyde, and the skeleton of Burke the Resurrectionist, were grisly company for my joyless mood. I had a wry memory of the comfort before exams – 'Golden lads and girls all must,/Like chimney-sweepers, come to dust' – afforded by other necrological things, the mummies in the Egyptian Gallery of the Royal Scottish Museum. I had recently learned that Leslie had left his regiment and was already on his way to the very land of the mummies.

It was at this time that I had my first contact with the world of the secret war, but with someone who could probably not have breached security even had he wanted to do so. My cousin, who had become a research scientist at Porton Down, the Chemical Warfare Establishment, asked me to entertain a Polish officer who had recently been attached to this station. Major Dowgiallo of the Polish Veterinary Corps was visiting Edinburgh, so my parents and I felt obliged to invite him to supper – a matter of no small thought in those days of food rationing. Major Dowgiallo could scarcely speak any English, and he had caused amusement when he had delivered a paper at Porton and found himself at a loss when discussing the decontamination of food on the hoof by means of applying bleaching powder. He was groping for the word to describe a sheep's fleece, and someone mischievously leaned over and whispered the word 'tunic'. With an appreciative 'Sankyouveymush', Major Dowgiallo continued for the rest of his talk to refer to 'the sheep's tunic', to the suppressed mirth of his audience. Each time he used the word 'tunic' he shot a grateful look at his perfidious interpreter.

I had heard this story, so I viewed the visit with some

apprehension. The major arrived, bearing the largest bouquet I had ever seen – in wartime it must have cost a king's ransom – red tulips and great white lilacs. This he presented to my mother with much hand-kissing and heel-clicking. Obtusely, we made our first gaffe by not recognising that these were the Polish national colours. Their sad history had made the Poles among the most chauvinistic of nations in the world. As the evening progressed its nightmarish quality increased. To say that conversation languished would be a gross understatement: it never flourished at all. Major Dowgiallo's English was minimal. (How good was our Polish?) Surprisingly, he had no French. I had never learned German, and my father's rudimentary knowledge of that tongue was long since forgotten. In desperation we found ourselves trying to exchange pleasantries in isolated words of *Latin*. I wondered if many in modern times (setting aside the Catholic Church, and the intellectual playfulness of university common-rooms) had tried to make an evening's light conversation in a dead language. This was not my first encounter with the Poles in a linguistic context. At the very start of the war, I came upon two Polish officers in a department store vainly trying to express their requirements to the giggling shop assistant. I asked whether they spoke French. This time they did, and we were able to sort out their problem – a request for new silver braid to sew onto their dazzling uniforms. For this trifling service I received quite disproportionate gratitude, and I saw how many British girls could be captivated (and some, alas, deceived) by such gallantry and charm; just as, later, many were attracted by the brash confidence and lavish spending of the Americans.

After a few weeks' not over-taxing work in the Anatomy Museum, I was summoned for interview to the Civil Service Commission in Burlington Gardens, London. The Board consisted of five men and one woman, and the grilling seemed to me in my nervousness a Spanish Auto de Fe. The first command was that I take off my hat so that they might see my eyes. Of all the questions they asked, one alone remains in my memory. It concerned my prowess at sport. As one who detested games and had been forced to play daily (and did so badly) at school – hockey, lacrosse, tennis and cricket – I was momentarily non-plussed. Then I dredged up from my memory my first eager term at university — a world ago it seemed — and my attempts at archery, which had appeared more attractive as an individualistic, and indeed antiquarian, skill, and freer of that tiresome team spirit against which I had been so well inoculated. So I served this more unusual offering up with the whimsical thought that to this highly traditional Board, meeting in embattled and war-scarred London, the spirit of Agincourt might not be inappropriate. I omitted to mention, however, that I had rarely got the arrow on the mark, being too slight and too weak of muscle to pull adequately on the bow. The Board must have been satisfied for, a week or so later, undoubtedly security-checked, I received an offer of an appointment in the Foreign Office. How glamorous and exciting it sounded!

Many years after the war, I learned that there was a school in Germany — very possibly more than one — which arranged for its pupils a network of pen-friends in various parts of Britain, and that, before delivery, the incoming letters were carefully combed by German Intelligence for minute personal and local details, such as where a family lived or whether the father had joined the Territorial Army, or been sent to work in a new factory. It transpired that British Intelligence had uncovered this spy system. However, nothing had been said about my correspondence with Gertrud Vieting, although I had no doubt at all that it was known.

Thus it was by this long and circuitous route that I came at length to Bletchley Station, and thence to Bletchley Park, and to learn the momentous nature of the work being done at Station X.

c

CHAPTER 6

What the Prime Minister said of Russia can equally apply to the Enigma code.

As far back as 1919 Hugo Koch, a Dutchman, envisaged an electrically-impulsed encoding machine. He called it by the splendid portmanteau name *Geheimschrijfmachine* – 'secret-writing machine'. In 1923 the Berlin engineer Arthur Scherbius developed the idea and named the product 'Enigma'. German Intelligence became interested and introduced Enigma into the navy in 1926; in 1928 it was adopted by the army, and by the air force in 1933, the year when Hitler came to power. It had meantime been withdrawn from the commercial market.

The Poles, with their historically danger-fraught position between Germany and Russia, had for some years been monitoring German military signals. Suddenly, in 1926, they were baffled, and they realised that the Germans were using a mechanical cypher. They responded by founding a small cryptology school at the University of Poznan.

The Enigma machine was of amazing complexity. It is really impossible for someone not technically qualified, or who was not at the time encouraged to understand more than a very limited aspect of its functions, to analyse the working of the apparatus. It is necessary to rely on the accounts published since the embargo on absolute secrecy was lifted in 1977, and there seems little advantage in repeating here what has been told so well already; and, after all, this book has quite a different purpose. It should, however, be enough to say that the Enigma machine looked like a large, clumsy, old-fashioned typewriter. Striking any letter caused a different letter to appear on another illuminated keyboard above. Peter Calvocoressi has described the principle of Enigma as succinctly as it is possible to do: 'The Enigma was an encyphering machine that produced a highly variable scramble of the 26 letters of the alphabet by passing electric current through a set of movable rotors, each of which by its internal electrical connections contributed to the overall scramble.'

Britain knew little about Enigma, but Captain Gustave Bertrand of the *Service de Renseignement* (the Intelligence Department of the French Secret Service) was in touch with the Poles. When, in July 1939, it seemed that war was inevitable, the Poles decided to give the French and the British the results of their research, as well as two actual Enigma machines. Bertrand, accompanied by Commander Alastair Denniston, head of the Government Code and Cypher School (GC & CS), and his assistant Dillwyn Knox, met with the Poles in a forest near Warsaw. The two machines, one for Britain and one for France, were handed over and it was to be Bertrand's responsibility to transport one to Paris and so on to London in the French diplomatic bag.

In August 1939 Denniston moved GC & CS from 54 Broadway, Westminster, to Bletchley Park, an ugly Victorian country house in Buckinghamshire. This was conveniently situated, being 50 miles from London and on the railway junction between Oxford and Cambridge – at a point (as Andrew Hodge, biographer of Alan Turing, one of BP's genius mathematicians, puts it) which was near the intellectual centre of England. To find suitable staff was a tremendous problem. Mathematicians of the finest calibre were essential for what then seemed the almost impossible task of breaking a code with astronomical permutations. There were some 50 different Enigma keys in use by the German army, navy and air force, and daily settings for each key. Sir Harry Hinsley in *British Intelligence in the Second World War* has summarised the awesome challenge: 'Instructions for arranging and setting the wheels could be changed as frequently as every 24 hours; anyone not knowing the setting was faced with the problem of choosing from 150 million, million, million solutions.'

The secret nature of the enterprise precluded advertising.

Recruiting, therefore, was for some time done by means of the Old Boy network. Someone knew a colleague (usually a Cambridge don) who would be highly valuable. Perhaps he had a friend of like rare quality . . . and so it went on. First World War codemen were recalled, and other exceptional younger men lured from the groves of academe. Like the Special Operations Executive, BP became (as M.R.D. Foot has said in his official history of SOE operations in France) a club with membership by invitation only. Thus early in the war, Bletchley became the intellectual centre of England in terms other than the purely geographical. Peter Calvocoressi has very acutely (if somewhat smugly) described the sort of people who worked at Bletchley – both brilliant high-flying code-breakers and the rank and file of graduate clerks milling round them:

> There were at BP Chiefs and Indians. The Chiefs in both areas – cryptography and intelligence – were distinguished from the Indians because they were fewer, preponderantly male and had better jobs – better because they were more responsible and closer to the brush of real events. But the Chiefs were not a different kind of person in the way that, in the armed services, officers were officers and men were men. The reason for this lay in the nature of the work done by the Indians . . . The *Ultra* community at BP saw itself as an élite within an élite . . . Nearly all of us had had the same sort of education and shared a common social background. We made, unwittingly for the most part, the same assumptions about life and work and discipline and values. Although we had never met before . . . we half-knew each other already. We fell into easy comradeship and collaboration. And these facts go some way to explain the astonishing further fact that the Ultra secret was kept not merely during the war, but for 30 years afterwards – a phenomenon that may well be unparalleled in history!

The intelligence derived from the Enigma machine – signals intelligence, known as SIGINT – was classified as Most Secret Ultra (or, as the Americans preferred to call it, Top Secret Ultra). To the code-breakers of Bletchley, to the Cabinet, the Chiefs of Staff and certain commanders in the field, this intelligence was referred to (as if to some rare commodity or magic panacea) as 'Ultra'. The first British decrypt was accomplished in the spring of 1940.

One of Ultra's early and dramatic successes concerned the invasion threat. In July 1940 Bletchley had intercepted a message from Goering to the chiefs of staff of the Luftwaffe in which was made clear Hitler's intention to prepare for the invasion of Britain – 'Operation Sea Lion', as it was code-named. Gist of this intelligence (with, of course, the utmost care to protect its source) must have been conveyed to all regional commands in the United Kingdom, and from there filtered downward, for this moment coincided with the time when Leslie declared his willingness to perform almost any task in order to help repel invaders. Meanwhile, our Photographic Reconnaissance Unit had observed an armada of barges assembled along the Dutch and Belgian coasts.

However, before any invasion attempt could take place, the RAF had to be put out of action, and on 8 August Goering issued his order of the day ('Operation Eagle'): a directive to the Luftwaffe to 'wipe out the RAF from the sky'. On 7 September an Alert No. 1 ('Cromwell') – i.e. invasion expected within 12 hours – was sent out in Britain, following the interception on 5 September of Goering's order for a mass raid on London docks, involving 300 bombers – a switch from the target of the battered airfields. Churchill was informed of this order within an hour, and watched the air raid from the Air Ministry roof. On 7 September the bombers struck at London itself – the real beginning of the Blitz – and on 9 September Ultra delivered a forecast of another 200-bomber raid on the city. It was following immediately upon this that, on 10 September, Leslie wrote me excitedly about a small enemy landing – a fact that was finally denied, and explained by Attlee in Parliament only in 1946. Leslie had stated that he actually saw a telegram saying that 'all had been caught', but this may have referred to the four spies which had been picked up near Rye in Kent.

During the Battle of Britain, Air Chief Marshal Dowding had the incomparable advantage of information from Ultra and he monitored its signals very carefully; he knew, therefore, that only 50 per cent of the German aircraft were then serviceable, and so, on 15 September he sent up every available fighter plane against the enemy. On 17 September Bletchley intercepted an order from Goering for the dismantling of loading equipment in Dutch aerodromes. This was rightly interpreted as meaning the abandonment of invasion plans – at least for that year.

A sad and ironic pendant to this story was the fact that when Dowding was dismissed he could not betray Ultra by calling it to the defence of his strategy.

Two further examples may show the effect of Ultra on the conduct of the war: the sinking of the *Bismarck* on 27 May 1941; and that critical moment in the Western Desert in August 1942 when Montgomery, through Ultra, was able to predict the direction and strength of Rommel's attack at Alam Halfa, where the Axis failure prepared then ground for the British success at El Alamein in the autumn.

There were also two occasions where Ultra appeared to fail – the bombing of Coventry on 14 November 1940, and the raid which caused the great fire of London in December of that year. These are both highly controversial instances: Winterbotham's pioneering account, Lewin's detailed study, and Calvocoressi's memoir disagree as to whether Coventry was sacrificed in order not to compromise the source of intelligence. I can say only that when I was at Bletchley the belief among my associates was that information had been received and that Ultra did not fail; the intelligence it provided could not be fully acted upon for fear of betraying Ultra itself. So far as I am aware, no writer on Ultra has noted the comparison between the Coventry affair and an episode in the First World War when secret intelligence was apparently neglected in order to protect the source. The German bombardment of Hartlepool and Scarborough in December 1914 was expected because of wireless intercepts. The Royal Navy moved to cut off the raiders, but fog allowed them to slip past. Churchill, as First Lord of the Admiralty, could not explain that he had been conscious of enemy intentions, without giving away the secret that German codes were being broken. Sir Alfred Ewing, head of Room 40 at the Admiralty, where the cryptography was carried on, was bemused that the Germans continued to use the codes which were already compromised, and he assumed that they considered arrogantly that the British were too stupid to break them. Likewise, in the Second World War, the Germans, perhaps because of their complacency, never realised that we were breaking the Enigma code. Rommel, indeed, put the blame on the Italians for leaking secrets: 'We know from experience,' he wrote in his diary, 'that Italian headquarters cannot keep things to themselves, and that everything they wireless to Rome gets to British ears.'

By the time I arrived at BP there was need for many more of those whom Peter Calvocoressi calls the Indians, and the net had been cast wider to trawl the less élite from universities other than Oxford and Cambridge. Following upon a letter written to Churchill by four senior cryptanalysts in Huts 6 and 8 complaining about the lack of resources, the Prime Minister had ordered that on 'extreme priority' Bletchley should have all that it needed. By the beginning of 1942 rapid expansion had taken place, so that by the end of that year there were some 3,293 staff of all grades, of whom 1,566 were service personnel and 1,727 civilian, and by the time that I had been there for a year there were over 5,000 in all.

```
He thought he saw a rattle snake
That questioned him in Greek.
He looked again and found it was
The middle of next week.
'But one thing I regret,' he said,
'Is that it cannot speak.'
        LEWIS CARROLL: 'SYLVIE AND BRUNO'
```

If Charles Dodgson had been alive during the Second World War he would have surely been recruited for Station X, not only for his mathematics but also for his amphigory. It was a 'Through-the-Looking-Glass' world. Edward Lear, too, would have felt at home in Bletchley's realm of Complete Nonsense; and he would even have found a friend called Foss. The platypus always seems a Lear-like creature; and the creator of that splendid rhyme

> I had a duck-billed platypus when I was up at Trinity,
> With whom I soon discovered a remarkable affinity . . .

was one of the denizens of Bletchley. One must remember, too, that Patrick Barrington's literary platypus was herself employed in the Foreign Office! Indeed the Enigma machine was a nonsense-maker in reverse. Of infinite complexity, it ingested gobbets of gobbledegook and disgorged segments of language which could be turned into coherent German.

To say that the terminology at BP was cryptic resembles the old lady's comment that she is suffering from a 'gastric stomach'; but there *was* an esoteric language to be learned. One talked of 'blisting', that is, making a list in the manner devised by a Mr Bannister – a 'B' list; or one 'fossed' when plotting a graph as Mr Hugh Foss decreed. 'The Dallae' referred to the identical Dallas twins who were consulted as the oracles of the Decoding Room School. The 'QR' was the Quiet Room, where specific researches were carried out – so called because of its distance from, and dissimilarity to, the Decoding Room where the clattering, devilish Enigma machine decrypted the intercepts received from nearby wireless stations.

In this strange institution we did not even know all the people who worked in the same room as ourselves, as the action went on 24 hours a day, and we were on duty on varying shifts. BP has been likened to a honeycomb where groups worked as if in sealed-off cells. We travelled the countryside by day and by night in buses, and were tumbled out of them in the blackout to grope our way 'home' through streets which, in their uniform monotony, were hardly distinguishable one from another, our torches, with their regulation double layer of tissue-paper over the bulb, showing like grounded fireflies in the intense darkness. As billetees, we lived *en famille* with people we had never previously met, who did not want our company and who did not know what we were doing in their towns. We had a terrific secret to guard; we could not speak – and that, at the beginning, was the hardest part.

I have a very clear recollection of Nigel de Grey, sometime Lieutenant-Commander in the Naval Intelligence Division during the First World War, giving us a lecture on security which was psychologically scarifying, as indeed it was meant to be. It was he who, with others in the legendary Room 40 at the Admiralty under the direction of Sir Alfred Ewing (later to be Principal and Vice-Chancellor of Edinburgh University), had decoded the famous Zimmermann telegram which played its part in bringing the United States into the First World War. Never, as long as we lived, he said, were we to mention to *anyone*, not our next-of-kin, not even those in other sections of the station, what was the nature of our work. This oath of secrecy I found so oppressive at first that I felt like the barber in the Greek myth who had to dig a hole in the ground and whisper, 'Midas has asses' ears!' But soon the consciousness of security became so ingrained that we lost all temptation to enquire about the nature of the work with which we were not immediately concerned.

(Sir) Frank Adcock, Professor of Ancient History at Cambridge and Fellow of King's, had also been in Room 40. He was recalled to GC & CS when it moved to Bletchley in 1939. The story was current when I was there that this distinguished classical scholar, so accustomed to dealing with the textual problems of Thucydides and Greek epigraphy, was somewhat disconcerted on arriving at Bletchley station to be greeted by an evacuee urchin, jeering: 'I'll read yer secret writing, guv'nor!'

My first sight of Bletchley Park was a very considerable disappointment. This was scarcely the country house of my dreams. For a start, it was not really a country house at all, rather a monstrosity on the edge of Bletchley town, with suburban dwellings stretching up to the gates. Devotees of Pevsner know, on opening a volume of *The Buildings of England*, to look for the section headed 'Perambulation' for whichever town or village in which they happen to find themselves. On modern Bletchley Sir Nikolaus's brevity is significant: 'There is no perambulation needed of Bletchley.' There was a *bon mot* current: one Foreign Office wit to another – 'I spent a month in Bletchley last Sunday'. The Park – itself unmentioned by Pevsner – had been built in the 1870s and greatly enlarged in the years after 1883. It was constructed of raw red brick with yellow stone dressings, in a style that was no style, but something resembling public-house Jacobean and lavatory-gothic, with a Kubla Khan dome from the Prince Regent's Brighton as a cultural stray added for good measure, and this cut one of the wooden gables in the most bizarre fashion. I suppose if one *had* to define the overall intention of the architect, one would say that he had built a pastiche in Tudor-Gothic. The wealth of Sir Herbert Leon, who had bought the Bletchley estate in 1883 and who set about transforming the house, was trumpeted loudly in the griffin statues on either side of the main entrance, in the exterior 'refinements', in the florid plasterwork of friezes and ceilings, and in the opulent oak panelling and heavily elaborate carved details of the interior. Leon was a stockbroker, a sometime Liberal MP for North Bucks, and a part-proprietor of the *Daily News*. But what is particularly interesting in the context of what his house became in the Second World War – and indeed what it is today, a Post Office

Engineering Training establishment – was his financial interest in the Anglo-American Telegraph Company.

★ ★ ★

On my arrival I was taken straight to sick bay where I was to spend the night, as a billet had not yet been found for me. I at once sensed the physical austerity and the quality of social and intellectual superiority characteristic of the best public schools. Unfortunately, I fell on the gravel, severely grazing my knee and, what was worse, ruining one of my two pairs of stockings – nasty rayon objects which sagged at the knees and cost precious clothing coupons. The matron of sick bay, a formidable lady by the name of Mrs de Courcey-Meade, painted my wound (unwashed) with gentian violet, and I had to suffer the embarrassment of meeting my colleagues with a tattered and fluorescent leg. It duly went septic.

I found no great welcome; people seemed quite oblivious of my arrival, and no doubt it was unconscious arrogance on my part to expect it to be otherwise. And yet, when I came to know my associates, a far greater intimacy and sense of comradeship developed than I had known with any but my closest friends at school or university.

Though irretrievably ugly, Bletchley Park was situated in pleasant enough grounds, well wooded, with specimens of many different varieties of trees. Ducks swam about on the lake, beside which we would sometimes sit of a summer evening after supper, before going back on duty. There was a ha-ha, and there had once been a maze: garden features which one might to represent the outside and inside views of BP as an institution! The establishment was ringed with barbed wire, and guarded by men of the RAF Regiment whose NCOs kept discipline by threatening their men that misdemeanours would result in their being sent 'inside the Park', as if it were some sort of madhouse.

All round the main building were wooden huts, and Hut 6, to which I was posted, was a large one about 60 feet long, divided by plasterboard partitions into several rooms, all of which contained the simplest and most basic furniture. I worked in Room 82, though in typical Bletchley fashion there were not 81 rooms preceding it. Hut 6 dealt with the recording of intercepts of German army and air force Enigma, and the decoding of them after the key of the day had been determined from the brilliant deductions of the code-breakers. (Hut 8 did the same for the German navy Enigma.) By the summer of 1942 the staff of Hut 6 were solving each day the settings of some 26 German army and air force keys – keys which themselves changed daily. A total output of about 25,000 army and air force decrypts per month from Hut 6 was increased to about 48,000 each month between the autumn of 1943 and the end of the war.

I was in the Decoding Room briefly, as were all Hut 6 recruits, but was very glad not to remain there, as the operators were constantly having nervous breakdowns on account of the pace of work and the appalling noise. From there I went to the Registration Room, where the intercepts were arranged in categories according to frequencies and call-signs. When the messages were decoded they emerged as apparently meaningless blocks of letters, and these were passed on to the linguists in Hut 3 who turned them into intelligible German. The translated intercepts were sifted, but not evaluated, and then submitted to the War Cabinet and the chiefs of staff. But all the information garnered was kept. Brian Johnson in *The Secret War* describes the volume of material with which Bletchley had to deal: 'Nothing was too small; everything, however trivial, was collated and filed in a huge card-index containing hundreds of thousands of names, units, postings, supply requisitions, details of promotions, courts martial and leave of absence. A transfer of a single Air Force lieutenant could reveal an impending attack. The card-index grew until it was virtually the archive of the entire German Command structure.'

Churchill relied heavily upon intelligence from Ultra, calling the Bletchley cryptanalysts 'the geese who laid the golden eggs but never cackled'; and he could frequently be heard demanding, 'Where are my eggs?' This glamour by association was a specious one. Very many tedious hours were spent on the dull and routine tasks of listing, plotting on graphs, meticulously checking and classifying. It was indeed amazing that the geese did not cackle; that so many young people held their peace and denied themselves the self-importance of being known to possess a supreme secret. It is equally astonishing that the Germans never guessed that we were breaking the Enigma code. Nor, it seemed, did they even suspect the existence of Station X. After all, Bletchley was an important railway junction, and the lines gleaming in the moonlight could have been an aid to enemy reconnaissance planes and bombers. Indeed, the RAF was known to use railway tracks as navigational guidelines. But the location's convenience for those Oxbridge dons who formed the nucleus of the original community had weighed down the scales against possible danger of discovery; and this judgement was vindicated, because we were never bombed. This was as well, for even a single light raid would have reduced the flimsy huts to matchwood. For our part, we appeared to take for granted the Germans' total ignorance of our presence, for we had no air-raid drill, nor did we have a single air-raid shelter, slit-trench, sandbag blast-wall, nor even so much as a steel helmet – only a large poster which read:

KEEP COOL AND CARRY ON

★ ★ ★

On the day after my arrival at Bletchley, I heard a Scottish voice and, being a little homesick, I sought out the owner. The voice belonged to Wendy Anderson, a St Andrews graduate, also a new girl, and as forlorn was I was. We discovered a strange fortuity: her mother and my father had been born in the same town of Dumfries and, moreover, we had a married connection – her cousin had married my cousin's cousin! 'My uncle,' said Wendy, expanding further on her family, 'was Provost of Dumfries; he had a rather odd name – "Chicken".' 'Not *Hen* Chicken?', I hazarded, as this humorous diminutive was part of my family mythology. Of course this sally and the discovery of our locational ancestry opened the way to friendship, though we soon realised that we had much more in common, not least a sharp sense of humour, which we were both going to need.

Work at BP went on 24 hours a day, in three shifts: 9 a.m. to 4 p.m., 4 p.m. to midnight, and midnight to 9 a.m., and added to this was the time spent in travelling to and from our billets some 20 miles away, which usually took just over an hour. Wendy and I were pleased to find that we were to be billeted in the same small town of Wolverton – pleased, that is, until we saw it! Twenty years after I was there – in the added bleakness of wartime and the blackout – the economist and educationalist John Vaizey (the late Lord Vaizey) was to write in an article in *Encounter*:

> Wolverton is a mid nineteenth-century railway town in Buckinghamshire, halfway between Oxford and Cambridge. There are hundreds of small hideous terrace houses in livid brick, a few chapels and railwaymen's clubs, humped in the flat countryside around the railway workshops and one of the most dangerous bridges in the country. It is a prosperous Southern edition of the squalid Northern Industrial town. The failure to rebuild it is somehow indicative of what is wrong with our country. Poised as it is, midway between the University cities, and on the main line to London, with the M1 only a few miles away, Wolverton seems like something out of *Fanny by Gaslight*. God knows what the North must be like, you feel, if Wolverton is like this!

To be strictly accurate, there are two Wolvertons, Old and New. Pevsner again is dryly acute: 'Old Wolverton the traveller does not notice, New Wolverton he cannot overlook.'

(New) Wolverton has now been modernised and, apart from a pleasant public library and some flower beds in the narrow residential streets, I do not think that the result is a great amelioration. The town is now part of the amorphous, dehumanised, characterless conurbation of Milton Keynes, where the roads in the green fields connecting the various centres of population are mere numbers on a grid. Among the 'improvements' is a sinister, rather frightening leisure centre and skateboard rink, the whole of a building-style resembling a huge aircraft hangar, and named with absurd pretension, 'The Agora'.

In 1942, to someone coming from Edinburgh with its romantic Old Town skyline of spires against hills, contrasting with the austere classical splendours of the Georgian New Town, Wolverton was something of a cultural shock. The streets ran in a regular criss-cross pattern sloping up from the railway works which lay behind a high camouflaged wall. This wall ran along one side of the Stratford Road and the residents called it 'The Front'. The railway works, established in mid-Victorian times to produce locomotives for the London and North-Western Railway, had shortly afterwards changed to the manufacture of carriages, most notably those for Royal trains, and 'made in Wolverton' was a byword for quality in coach building. Delving into the local history of the area, I discovered with amusement that in the early 1850s a certain superintendent of the then London & Birmingham Railway works at Wolverton had designed a fast new locomotive. These, as a class, were soon nicknamed 'Bloomers'. This alluded to contemporary sartorial developments in America, where Mrs Amelia Bloomer had pioneered somewhat daring cycling costumes for ladies which revealed their lower limbs. The Wolverton engines, shorn of 'the decent skirting of an outside frame exhibited all the wheels to the traveller's gaze'. 'The Works' – as we came to know the railway shops – provided most of the employment for the local inhabitants. Many of the remainder were absorbed by McCorquodale the printers. My billetor Mrs Webster told me that she had been employed there before her marriage and 'printed registered envelopes in two sizes for ten years, and liked the work'.

In the Wolverton of 1942 there was no library, no café, no bookshop, no cinema, and thus an unsophisticated Scots girl who would never at home have entered a public house often found herself of an evening among Bletchley friends in The Galleon, an inn overlooking the Grand Junction Canal at Old Wolverton, where the brightly painted barges plied up and down from London to Manchester, and noting how different was the English pub from the uncouth male preserve that was its Scottish counterpart. The Galleon had formerly been named The Locomotive. It seemed that the local inhabitants had betrayed their past for the sake of the fictitious glamour which the new name was imagined to convey. Wolverton meant railways and, earlier in our industrial past, canals and narrow-boats: but never the Spanish Main!

My landlady, Mrs Webster, was a woman with a sharp nose and a thin mouth; her iron-grey hair was cut in a clubbed bob and she wore round, thin-rimmed spectacles; her uniform was a cross-over apron. If at first I was disconcerted by her appearance, she was no less surprised by mine. Since I came from Scotland she had expected me to be 'large, raw-boned and "dower" [i.e. dour]'. But in spite of her slightly forbidding looks, Mrs Webster was kind, if in a rather unimaginative way. She was intensely house-proud, though her home was mean and small, having a frontage of not more than 12 feet, and opening directly on to the street, with no garden before it. She boasted that she had *two* bedrooms *and* a bathroom, which had been constructed from a third bedroom. Indeed it was cause for pride in this area. The WC, however, was outside, and I used to indulge in a small secret smile when, having crept out on a freezing night to the little 'necessary house', I must needs sit facing an outdated calendar showing a picture of 'A Sunny Haven'.

I had a room to myself but, because fuel was rationed, there was no heating in it, and so in my time off I was forced to sit with Mr and Mrs Webster. He was a gentle man, happily dominated by his competent wife. I used to find my bed set at an angle from the wall, and though I straightened it, always it was moved back into this odd position. Eventually Mrs Webster explained that she had had an evacuee before me, who had 'breathed on the wall', and she did not want me to do likewise.

Our lodging was not free, as it was for our service colleagues; we paid one guinea a week, and five shillings for transport (which we could scarcely avoid), and a fixed regular sum for meals necessarily taken in the canteen at BP. Nor did we receive travel warrants for our three-monthly seven-day leaves; and in those days when civilian travel was frowned upon we had no uniform to prove that our journey was really necessary. These anomalies caused not a few petty grouses. Our billetors were obliged to provide us with breakfast, which might be taken about 7.30 (or 10.30 if we had been on night duty), and one other meal which had also to be a movable feast. This must have been irksome for them, but Mrs Webster accepted it as her war work with good grace. Our third meal we ate while on duty – sometimes at 2 a.m. – in the huge cafeteria erected just outside the gates of the Park. The food was not particularly appetising – I remember with especial distaste the packeted pastry fruit pies which we called 'cardboard tarts' – but then, few expected delectable food in wartime. Some people, though, were very hungry, and second helpings were not allowed. I recollect one girl putting on dark glasses as a disguise in the hope that she would be luckier than Oliver Twist. She was similarly rebuffed. One of our diversions was to take coffee after supper in the station buffet. It was a gloomy place, almost a replica of the film set for *Brief Encounter*. But nothing so romantic ever transpired there, and the coffee was as bad as railway coffee has always been, and much worse than it is now. I cannot imagine why we chose this post-prandial pleasure, except that it was the only place available as a change from the BP cafeteria. For my part, I think there was the temptation to cause myself pain: to call up the memory of so many anguished parting at railway stations, so much less anguished (it seemed now) than the final one. Perhaps I was luxuriating in

> All the sadness in the sweet,
> The sweetness in the sad.

Or perhaps it was that recollection, however poignant, was better than emptiness.

Our billetors were obliged, wherever possible, to provide us with one bath per week; where this was not possible, facilities were available at BP, but this interfered with transport provisions, and sometimes a request for private transport was necessary, though not readily granted, and arrangements for this were in the hands of a Mrs Wildboar-Smith. The obligation of the bath Mrs Webster never failed to observe, though she did not trust me to keep to the statutory four inches, but ran the water in for me, adding, in spite of my protests, a most nauseous soap powder. Hairwashing had to be performed in cold water, which was very unsatisfactory, and in winter positively painful. When I came home about 1.30 a.m. after evening shift, I had the choice of a hot-water bottle or a hot drink. I did not think to emulate Mr Gladstone, who is reputed to have put tea in a stone 'pig' and then drunk it after the chill had been taken off the sheets. I was very lucky, though, to be given a key; some of my colleagues had to rouse both the bodies and the ire of their landlords at this unsocial hour. The stair of my billet creaked, however, and no matter how carefully I tiptoed, in the morning I was always greeted with, 'We heard you come in last night', and of course I felt guilty, especially as we could not defend ourselves, having to pretend that our work was of little account. In this we must have succeeded, for I marvelled at our billetors' ready assumption of it. Indeed, the Websters used to contrast me, quite without malice, with 'people who work'. Complaints were made, however, by some of the local residents about the 'do-nothings' of Bletchley Park.

Because of clothes rationing, fashion was abandoned but vanity not totally so. Stockings were discarded altogether, but we painted our legs (sometimes complete with 'skeuomorphic' seam) with a powdery liquid which was extremely difficult to wash off, especially in cold water. Travelling by bus at night in winter could be a chilling experience, so my mother made me anklets from the fur cuffs of an old coat; these stayed on by means of snap fasteners, and I must have looked like a poodle, but they provided considerable comfort.

Getting medical attention was a problem for us at BP. Unlike the service personnel, we civilians did not have our own medical officer. Indeed, on the part of the authorities there was an attitude of ignoring our welfare. The Billeting Office found us accommodation, but no one appeared to be responsible for us otherwise, though I expect we could have gone to our administrative chief Harold Fletcher, if we had been in any serious trouble. We had therefore to find our own medical adviser. In Wolverton there were two doctors. One had the reputation of being always drunk, and the other was a Scotsman, which was not necessarily a different thing. However, Wendy and I felt it safer to choose the Scotsman – perhaps, also, because, away from home Scots notoriously become clannish. But I soon found that this had been a dubious choice. The doctor had a mother-in-law who guarded his surgery like a fire-breathing dragon. The hour of the evening consultation was posted up on the doctor's door as being 6 p.m.; no final time was mentioned. I went along one night at 6 p.m. precisely, to be turned away by the dragon because 'there is no surgery tonight, as no patients have come'. '*I* have come,' I ventured to say, but the mother-in-law briskly discounted me as a person, and would not let me see the doctor. It was a rather worrying situation, as we had absolutely no other access to medical help. I feared that even an emergency home call might go unheeded.

I dreaded night duty: not in itself, for the night watch in our room was a small and generally friendly one. There were three of us, a man and (for propriety!) *two* girls. This ratio was especially desirable on those nights when a certain ex-journalist called Eric was on duty, making suggestive and tedious jokes. We kept awake with cups of cocoa, which was off the ration. We found cocoa very comforting, and quite deprecated Chesterton's rhyme:

> Tea although an Oriental
> Is a gentleman at least;
> Cocoa is a cad and coward,
> Cocoa is a vulgar beast.

My problem was that I could not sleep during the day. Of course we had no right to expect the life of the household, let alone the street, to be hushed because of us, but in the absence of quiet it took me hours to drift off. There was also the necessity of waking up in time to catch the transport to work. Alarm clocks were unobtainable, so I had brought one from home, antiquated and enormous, with a bell like a fire-alarm, and I used to lie tense and rigid waiting for it to ring. After my first spell of night duty I collapsed into bed and slept for 19 hours. Mrs Webster said that she came into my bedroom several times, fearing I might be in a coma!

The Websters were decent, reasonable people. Not all were so fortunate with their billetors. Wolverton was an area of narrow Nonconformist faith, and our comings and goings at strange times were viewed by some with disapproval and suspicion, especially since we could not really explain the necessity for the shift work. There was no attempt to match billetor and billetee – finding accommodation for the growing numbers at BP was too difficult and too vital for such niceties to be observed. One of my friends, Elizabeth Brockhurst, a Catholic convert, was billeted on Plymouth Brethren: she was not permitted to play her wireless, as it was considered a contraption of the Devil. Once, she obtained from her landlady special dispensation to hear a performance of *Messiah*, but the landlord hummed hymns throughout in order to register his disapproval. He had the habit of singing joylessly about the house, and my colleague was one day amazed to hear what she thought was 'Drink to me Only'; she had, however, little time to be surprised at this sensuality, for more careful listening revealed that the words were all about hell-fire and damnation.

At some point during my stay in Wolverton there arose a rumour that the church of St James in the neighbouring railway workers' village of New Bradwell had not been consecrated for the performance of weddings. New Bradwell was a depressing and hideous settlement of tiny brick terraces, scarcely recognisable as a conventional village. Life here, which was dingy enough with war conditions overlying the natural drabness of environment and narrowness of mind, was suddenly galvanised into alarm by the thought that half the population might not be decently married at all. This crisis – believed, through ignorance of what really constituted a legal marriage, to be of world-shaking dimension – further compounded the prevailing atmosphere of gloom. Sympathy for the predicament in which the New Bradwell folk thought themselves to be, spread round the district. Mrs Webster, though not entirely sure that they were unnecessarily worried, pitied their anxiety none the less.

A friend of the Websters' son (who was in the Middle East) took to visiting the house rather often, and one evening he asked me to go with him to the cinema in Bletchley. I had no wish to do so, but neither did I want to hurt his feelings. I tried to make my excuse sound plausible, but I fear I *did* hurt him; he had been pronounced unfit for military service and he was lonely and smarting at his exclusion from the experience of his peers. I think now that I need not have been so prim and stand-offish, but I was afraid to wound him further by giving him what might possibly be taken for false 'encouragement'.

Sometimes, travelling back from work in the moonlight, I would allow myself to fall silent and to wonder what scenes this moon was shining on in the Western Desert, where I had learned that Leslie now was; and whether he was in present danger. And I would realise with a pang that I had forfeited my right to concern. So I would endeavour to push these thoughts away. I was growing in emotional courage, and I had the rather wry thought that Leslie would have been proud of me.

★ ★ ★

Bletchley Park has been called a menagerie, and in the variety and eccentricity of his inhabitants, so it was. It had now cast its net more widely over the British universities for the most brilliant mathematicians, physicists and chess-players it could find; and some from other disciplines and of diverse talents had been trawled.

The story is told that a certain academic was recruited as an expert (supposedly) on cryptograms, when in actuality he was an authority on crypto*gams*. This mistake having been brought to light, perhaps the recruit was also a secret bigamist, someone wisecracked, making yet more play out of the two Greek words which formed the terminology of the newcomer's subject of study. Botanist though he was proved to be, nevertheless he stayed. *Chambers Dictionary* defines 'cryptogams' as a 'class of flowerless plants so named by Linnaeus in the expectation that sexual reproduction would one day be discovered'. The dramatic irony was further heightened when it was revealed that the botanist and would-be cryptographer was indeed engaged in an extra-marital affair.

Of all the Bletchley eccentrics I suppose the most celebrated now must be Alan Turing, largely because he has been the subject of Hugh Whitemore's very successful play *Breaking the Code*. Turing's idiosyncracies were legendary. His preferred method of transport from his billet to BP was by bicycle. The chain was faulty and came off at regular intervals. Rather than bear the cost and inconvenience of having it put right, he would count the revolutions of the pedals and would dismount exactly in time to adjust the chain manually. A true story – albeit hard to believe – was that, fearing the devaluation of the currency, he had melted down a considerable quantity of silver coin and buried the ingots in the ground of the Park. Unfortunately he could never remember where.

In one of my close acquaintances at BP, rationing and shortages to effect an eccentric metamorphosis. She developed a compulsive need to accumulate vast stocks of whatever attractive goods were available 'under the counter'. An allowance from her father over and above her paltry salary enabled her to buy these commodities whenever, and indeed wherever, they were available. For example, she considered Yardley's Foundation Cream highly desirable, and would purchase it at every shop where it was to be found, with the consequence that she must have had dozens of pots stored, all drying up, in the limited accommodation provided in her billet. This bizarre characteristic did not disappear with the end of the war, for when I visited her home during a sugar shortage in the 1970s, I saw the dining-room mantelpiece piled high with two-pound bags – enough, surely, to satisfy the most desperate sweet-tooth for months, or even years, to come.

Two members of the WAAF posted to Station X neatly encapsulated the idiosyncratic nature of Bletchley Park and its denizens in these verses, which I found with great pleasure in Beryl Escott's *Women In Air Force Blue*:

> I think that I shall never see
> A sight so curious as BP.
> This place called up at war's behest,
> And peopled with the queerly dressed,
> Yet what we did we could not say
> Nor ever shall till judgment day.

> The Air Force types who never fly,
> Soldiers who never do or die,
> Land-lubber sailors, beards complete,
> Long-haired civilians, slim, effete.
> Why we were there we never knew,
> And if we told, it wasn't true.

> For five long years our war was there
> Subject to local scorn and stare.
> We came on foot, by coach or train,
> The dull, the brilliantly insane.
> What were we for? Where shall we be,
> When peace at last demobs BP?

At Bletchley were two Professors of the University of Edinburgh, Alexander Aitken and Walter Bruford, who had left their chairs of Mathematics and German respectively to devote their appropriate talents to more urgent intellectual tasks. There were many others, not mathematicians or academic linguists, whose function I did not know (and not all of whom I met in what was by then a large organisation), who became celebrated in later life. These were just some among the denizens of BP: Angus Wilson, the novelist; Alan Pryce-Jones, later to become editor of *The Times Literary Supplement*; J.H. Plumb, destined to be the Professor of Modern English History at Cambridge and Master of Christ's; Roy Jenkins; Asa Briggs, future Vice-Chancellor of Sussex University and subsequently Provost of Worcester College, Oxford; and Dorothy Hyson, representing the theatre. There was a Captain Dennis Babbage whose hobby was *Bradshaw*, the famous railway timetable; and anyone who had a journey to make was welcome to consult him about the easiest (or most interestingly complicated) route to take. There seemed to be a high proportion of classical scholars – Denys Page, Hugh Last and T.B.L. Webster among them – which was not surprising given the traditional Civil Service preference for the logical mind associated with the products of Greats or the Cambridge Classical Tripos. Enoch Powell was involved with Ultra through a Special Liaison Unit (SLU) in the Middle East. (There were seven of these, whose function was to convey information gained through Ultra to the Allied High Commands in various parts of the world.) The list of distinguished old Bletchley hands is lengthy indeed, and at the bottom of the pile was the clutch of young graduates like me. Scions of the aristocracy also infiltrated – a descendant of Chatham for one; and when a girl whom I knew only as Meriel remarked, as we were washing up the cocoa cups, that she was 'brought up in a bog', and I commented naïvely that she had no trace of Irish accent, the unassuming daughter of the Earl of Meath merely smiled.

★ ★ ★

There were two girls in my room in Hut 6 who drew my admiration. Both were already war widows – little Anne Raymond, rosy-cheeked, with too-bright eyes, which when glimpsed unwary were full of sorrow. Anne could often be heard singing, with pathetically resolute cheerfulness bent to the occasion, 'Praise the Lord, and pass the ammunition'. The other girl was Angela Woodin, flaxen-haired, quiet, kind and stoical. I looked on these two girls with awe, and shuddered to think what it would be like to be in their position.

Then there was blonde and bubbly Joan Pyman, who always wore baby blue to match her eyes. Her fiancé seemed to be on a Cook's tour of the Middle East, and she had a touching faith in my opinion as to his current safety. She would rush up to me with, 'Gus is in Syria! Is that all right?' Alas, I never knew whether Gus survived to come home and marry her. I spent a day with her family at Eastbourne – except that it wasn't *with* her family, for I hardly met them. I thought the occasion an amalgam of a Noël Coward comedy and an Aldwych farce. People drifted in and out, not acknowledging one's presence, and my only meeting with Joan's mother was when she rushed past me with a vague smile and a tennis racquet. The hospitality I was used to in Scotland may not have been so lavish, but it was certainly warmer and more personal.

* * *

Gordon Welchman in *The Hut Six Story* tells an amusing yarn about the man who took over the administration of the 'highly intelligent female staff' of the Decoding Room and the Registration Room, and whom I grew to know quite well:

> My old school and university friend Harold Fletcher came to us . . . via the army, but his story was somewhat more complicated . . . He wrote to me to say that his occupation would become 'unreserved' on August 1, 1941, but that his firm would only release staff to join the armed forces. So, no doubt as a result of some string-pulling from Bletchley, Harold's local recruiting office was instructed by the War Office to recruit him into the Intelligence Corps. When he reported for the necessary swearing and documentation, the local recruiting officer and his staff were understandably

disappointed that Harold could tell them nothing about what his duties were to be. The sergeant's parting shot was, 'I supposed you'll be in the desert in a few weeks' time disguised as a Bedouin.' On August 6 . . . he reported to an officer in London and was told that he was just in time to catch the 3.06 p.m. train to Bletchley where he would be met by someone. Sure enough, someone met him and took him to the adjutant of No. IV Intelligence School who immediately made arrangements for a billet in nearby Linslade. From what he heard of the telephone conversation, Harold gathered that the billetor was unwilling to have a private soldier and had to be persuaded that this particular specimen knew how to behave. Harold's military career lasted some eight months. He was at once promoted to lance-corporal but although Travis [Commander Edward Travis who was chief administrator at BP] tried for the next six months to find a suitable military unit to which Harold could be attached as an officer, he had no luck. However, at that point, Harold's firm changed its rules, allowing him to be 'demobbed', placed on W reserve, and employed for wartime duties by the Foreign Office. Of course he had been working for Hut 6 from the day of his arrival at Bletchley and his duties soon became important. He only wore uniform when going on leave (in order to get a cheap fare). Otherwise he concealed the fact that he was in the army as far as possible.

Few of us in Hut 6 ever knew that our revered chief was a mere lance-corporal!

Most of the brains of the organisation, or those academics who were able to pull Establishment strings and make the best of college connections, were billeted fairly comfortably near BP or had private transport, and were therefore able to take part in the social life that was organised for the community. For those of us who lived farther afield and were dependent on buses, such participation was seldom possible. I do remember, however, attending a Christmas revue in 1942 which was held in a hall near the Park. Group Captain John Shephard, who commanded the wireless intelligence station at Chicksands

Priory in Bedfordshire, where many of our intercepts were received, was invited to one such entertainment and reported upon 'a performance whose brilliance was undiminished by having to appeal to an audience whose IQ was not less than 200'! The show was worthy of the Cambridge Footlights, and I have no doubt that some of the participants had been members of that renowned dramatic society. Enjoying this recreation, I could not banish the occasional thought that although work at BP was undeniably of vital importance, we were living a comparatively sheltered life, and that the real brunt of the war was being borne by the men on the battlefield. The contribution of Ultra to the conduct of the war both in terms of grand strategy and in individual operations was incalculable; and its real role is still being assessed. But in the final analysis, things had not changed since Wellington had pointed to a British infantryman before Waterloo with the words 'It all depends on that article'.

CHAPTER 8

I agree with Juvenal. I cannot altogether agree with Ruskin. My thirst
for real travel was to have its very modest beginnings on the railways
of the Midlands when I was at BP. My journeying consisted of little
trips to neighbouring towns within a radius of 50 miles north, south,
east and west of Bletchley. And being indeed penniless gave me a
curious and delightful feeling of freedom. An account of these travels
will appear tame indeed unless one realises the extreme limitations
imposed by shift work, penury and wartime restrictions. Narration of
some pathetically parochial journeys seems almost naïve now, but then
such 'travels' were a welcome relief from the tensions of BP, and the
dreariness of billeting.

Stony Stratford was the town nearest to Wolverton, and by
comparison it had considerable charm. It lay on Roman Watling
Street, and had two old coaching inns, each with enormous, elaborate
wrought-iron signs which stretched halfway across the road. These
were The Cock and The Bull, and anecdotes arising out of their
proximity and rivalry were said to have given rise to the phrase 'cock
and bull story'.

I began to use the mornings of those days when I was on evening watch for these little sorties, and covered quite a bit of territory – Leighton Buzzard, High Wycombe, Buckingham, Dunstable, Newport Pagnell, Woburn, Banbury, Northampton, Aylesbury, Bedford, and even as far as Whipsnade and the Chiltern Hills. Many of the excursions I made with Wendy Anderson who had become a close friend. Summer outings the next year were for her a misery. She suffered dreadfully from hay fever, and many were the times – such as when we picnicked on Ivinghoe Beacon – she would have benefited from emulating Alan Turing who was said to cycle to work wearing an army gas-mask to protect himself from the pollen.

I had been to London on comparatively few occasions before coming to Bletchley, and it was still to me a place of awe and wonder. I could not go there very often, however, for such an expedition cost a week's salary. The fare was 10 shillings (50p), and then there was lunch, often taken at one of the new mass-market eating-places, such as the Quality Inns, which had sprung up no doubt to satisfy the American GIs' taste in food: 'Aunt Mary's Home-made Apple Pie' was constantly on the menu. There was the lure of the big stores, though clothing coupons and shortage of money made them a feast for the eye only. I was in London on 8 March 1943, the night of the Bethnal Green tube-station tragedy. At the sound of the air-raid siren, a woman carrying a child tripped at the entrance to the Underground, and a panic-stricken crowd pushed in behind her; 173 people were trampled to death. This was not an area I was likely to visit but, nevertheless, my poor mother, hearing the report on the wireless, was sure that I must be among the casualties! Music and the theatre flourished as an escape from austerities and anxieties. With Wendy I went to at least one of the famous lunchtime concerts organised by Dame Myra Hess at the National Gallery. We had persuaded our landladies to give us packed lunches in place of the statutory second meal. When Wendy opened hers, she found that it consisted entirely of crispbread and realised that she would be able to eat only during the applause – Harrison Birtwhistle's music had not yet been written.

We had one free day each week – any one of our choice – and we could also elect to work for 12 days consecutively and then have two days off. We discovered the trick of working two watches together –

4 p.m. till midnight and midnight till 9 a.m., and then taking the morning train to Scotland. This saving of time, together with our two days' leave, gave us a full 48 hours at home. We travelled back overnight and went straight on duty. Those journeys were a nightmare. The lights in the train were a dim, depressing blue, and every space was crammed with servicemen and their kit; they crowded the corridors, and lay in the luggage-racks, which being (in Dr Johnson's phrase) 'reticulated and decussated, at equal distances, with interstices between the intersections' made passable network hammocks. The troops also slept in the lavatories – a very awkward situation, this, as sometimes, if there was an air-raid, the train crawled and the journey could take as long as 16 hours. In those conditions there was no place for what H.E. Bates called 'the air of silent refrigeration, the arid cross-examination of stares'; the war had 'smashed the silence', for long the hallmark of railway travel in Britain. Wendy went to Glasgow and had a direct trip; I had to change at Rugby on the way north and at Carstairs coming south. This was surely the coldest and draughtiest station in the country, and I always had to wait there about midnight; and I used to pray that the train would stop with a door opposite to me, so that I should have some chance of getting on at all. The servicemen were always very helpful in hauling one aboard, but I was not in uniform and I always felt they must be wondering whether or not I had any right to travel.

★ ★ ★

I had become friendly with Vivien Fish, whose father was Churchill's dentist. I declined an invitation to have him fill a tooth, because I felt that I should never be able to afford the fee; but I did accept the offer to be shown by Vivien round Oxford (or 'Hoxford' as Mrs Webster called it, with that superfluous Beds. and Bucks. 'h' which is often a wrongly omitted 'h' in other parts of England). Vivien had been up at St Hugh's, so I was looking forward to her being an excellent guide. Oxford was my Xanadu. It was for me a phantom of literary delight; a name, though less euphonious, almost as evocative as Samarkand, Trebizond or Persepolis. The dreaming spires had etched themselves deeply on my imagination. We stayed at the Golden Cross, an old coaching inn in the Cornmarket, and this in itself enchanted me, with its charm of sloping floors and crooked beams. I learned to refer to 'the High', 'the Broad' and 'the Turl' – where I bought, with a guilty spurt of loyalty to my own country, an antique 'Map of the South Part of Scotland'. We visited Blackwell's, such a bookshop as I had never before seen, and Vivien left with armfuls of books, and I, happy with one modest Penguin. I marvelled at the stone coloured like golden honey, the crockets and pinnacles, the needle-points aspiring to heaven, the bosses and badges blazoned in *gules, azure, or* . . . it was all very heady stuff.

Vivien had some friends still up at Oxford and had arranged to meet them for lunch at the Randolph Hotel. I excused myself in order to explore. After a while I sat down in a secret place by the Cherwell and fell to musing about how I had once myself aspired to Oxford, how one of my lecturers at Edinburgh had urged me to go on to read for a B.Litt there, but of course the war had put an end to any such ambitions. Still, however, I cherished the fantasy that I might one day have a son who would fulfil that dream, and always he had Leslie's eyes, dark, with soft expressive light. But I would not see Leslie again. It was just before the Battle of Alamein – Bletchley was providing Montgomery with vital intelligence – and, had I but known it, Leslie was, almost at that same moment, listening on the wireless to 'One Fine Day', and suffering because he thought he would never see *me* again. Neither was I to know that I should indeed one fine day have a son who would make me very proud of him at the 'Other Place', but that it would be from green eyes that the light of intelligence and wit would shine.

I stood on Magdalen Bridge in the dying day, and the sky, mother-of-pearl streaked with violet and awash with rose and yellow light, gave me a tightness at the throat; it seemed an intimation of all the beauty and sorrow of the world.

Then I went to Cambridge, and fell in love all over again with its more flaunting charms. The Backs enchanted me, and I thought that there could surely be no lovelier ecclesiastical building in the country, and perhaps all Europe, than King's Chapel, with its perfect fan-vaulting and its jewelled windows staining with glorious blue the white-gold stone. I gazed in admiration at the splendid mellow brick

Tudor gatehouses of Trinity and St John's with their painted coats of arms and their octagonal towers; at the oriel windows, and the fantastically-patterned corkscrew chimneys; at the playful Gothic-revival fantasy of the Bridge of Sighs. A pilgrimage to Grantchester proved a literary disappointment. The Old Vicarage and Byron's Pool seemed hardly worth Brooke's eulogy. This was the first occasion when I experienced the disillusion of actually seeing a place I had come to love through a poem – that had been, in Drinkwater's phrase, 'lissom in a dream'.

When my mother and a friend came to visit me at Wolverton I brought them to Cambridge and, with the confidence of inexperience, I took them punting on the river. Of course I got into difficulties, and was rescued by a kindly and condescending undergraduate. I always looked very young for my age and from his manner I suspected he thought I was a schoolgirl. To excuse my ineptitude I did not enlighten him. That same year when visiting my cousin, stationed in Wiltshire, I was aware that one of his friends was 'talking down' to me. It transpired that Gilbert, always a joker, had said that I was 14; I was, in fact, 23.

By Christmas 1942 I had settled down pretty well at BP. I had made friends and was enjoying the camaraderie that was peculiar to wartime organisations. To an only child, this sense of community was especially satisfying. I was not, however, very happy in Wolverton. My billetors were kind, but I had to spend considerable time in their sitting-room, and I felt this was an invasion of privacy for both of us. As a Scot, I was expected to take New Year's Day as leave rather than Christmas. The Websters, in spite of rationing, produced a formidable midday Christmas dinner. A fire was lit in the 'front room' (the only time I had known it to be used). They did their best to include me as 'family', but I felt rather forlorn and sad, so far from those I loved, and from one especially, not only in distance but in spirit. After dinner Mr and Mrs Webster retired to the 'front room' to sleep off the meal, and I was glad to be going on evening watch, which I believed would help to dispel my sense of isolation.

★ ★ ★

Wendy and I saved up two days' leave for New Year, and we decided to spend it with my cousin, through whom we had the marriage connection. A research scientist at the Chemical Warfare Establishment at Porton Down, he was living in the village of Pitton, seven miles from Salisbury. The journey was enlivened by the presence in our compartment of a drunken Scotsman. The train had no corridor, each compartment having doors opening directly to the outside. Our sole companion had been drinking heavily, with inevitable consequences. It was obvious that he was becoming increasingly uncomfortable, and no station was due with facilities for relief; and in the blackout the train crawled exasperatingly. Eventually it stopped in the middle of nowhere. Our fellow-traveller had been mumbling for some time that he would 'hae tae get oot!'. Now he saw his chance and desperation forced him to take the risk of climbing down on to the line in the darkness. Wendy and I were at once amused and embarrassed, but also concerned lest he be mown down by a passing train. However, we were relieved (though not as much as he) to see his face, grinning inanely, as he climbed back in through the window.

We arrived very late and, through some misunderstanding, Gilbert was not at the station to meet us. We waited a very long time in growing unease. However were we going to get to Pitton in the blackout? There were few buses at any time, and none at that hour. I did not know Salisbury well enough – Wendy did not know it at all – to grope my way to an hotel (and, anyhow, we feared we had not enough money for a bed). We were discussing the necessity of spending the night in the station waiting-room when we saw a taxi. It seemed a forlorn hope that any taxi-driver, especially with the limitation of petrol-rationing, should consider a fare which would take him seven miles out of the town on New Year's Eve, but incredible luck was with us! The taxi-driver had been born in Glasgow – our second compatriot of the night – and he took pity on 'two wee Scotch lassies' and drove us all the way for a very modest remuneration. Never had we been so pleased to see a house and a coal fire, and to have a warm welcome!

Daylight showed us that we were in an idyllic sixteenth-century thatch-roofed cottage, set in the immemorial rolling Wiltshire countryside. And we spent two blissful days far from the stresses of war-news, work and the irritations of transport and billeting. We could almost have forgotten about the war but for the shell-holes in the surrounding downland, stark white chalk amid the tawny grass, the result of gunner practice on the artillery and tank ranges at Tidworth, Bulford and at Larkhill, where I remembered Leslie had gone to a firing camp all those months ago. There was also the presence of land-girls on neighbouring farms to remind Wendy of her own few months in the Women's Land Army at St Andrews, where many Polish troops were stationed. A certain officer used to linger, 'chatting her up'. On one occasion she was engaged in a particularly back-breaking task, and her shrewd sense of humour observed the struggle between his dignity as a Polish officer and his chivalry as a gentleman. Eventually, chivalry won, and he took off his jacket to help. When caught in the act by one of his fellow officers, he hastened to justify himself: 'She ees zo leetle, and ze vork ees zo harrt.'

We were always hungry in wartime. When one looks back, it is with amazement that survival on the meagre rations was possible. On a recent visit to the Imperial War Museum to see the new display relating to the Home Front, I could scarcely believe that the tiny quantities of food represented by the plastic replicas were really the weekly allowances by which we kept together body, soul and fighting spirit. At Pitton during this New Year interlude we were able to satisfy some of our suppressed gastronomic longings by the intemperate consumption of farm eggs, butter and cheese – off the ration, at times, in the country – and also of decontaminated sugar, salvaged from poison-gas experiments at Porton Down, and used to make excellent 'tablet', as we call it in Scotland. We asked my cousin if the poor laboratory rats had 'gone for a Burton', and the sally caused to flit across our minds a phrase from *The Anatomy of Melancholy* condemning gluttony as 'the source of all our infirmities and the fountain of all our diseases'. We resolutely refused to be scourged by it, and ate the ill-gotten confectionery all the same.

CHAPTER 9

O joy of love's renewing
  Could love be born again.
Relenting of thy rueing
  And pitying my pain;
O joy of love's awakening,
  Could love arise from sleep,
Forgiving and forsaking
  The fields we would not reap.
ANDREW LANG: SONG FROM *THE WORLD'S DESIRE*

I kept up a close correspondence with my parents, partly because I knew that they missed me and partly from natural inclination and affection. One day in February 1943 I returned to my billet to find the usual envelope addressed in my mother's round handwriting. I registered only the habitual glow of pleasurable comfort, but when I opened the envelope the reaction was one of electric shock. There fell out an air-letter in a once very familiar hand. I am afraid I did not pause to read my mother's letter, but tore open the enclosure with spastic fingers. The words quivered on the page: 'You will probably be surprised at this letter,' Leslie wrote. 'Among the few books I took with me into the desert was *The Oxford Book of Modern Verse* which you gave me. I often used to read it when we were in action and, believe it or not, every time I took up the book it opened at page 92, although I have never deliberately read that page, as far as I can remember – so I took the hint and wrote . . .'

I always had several anthologies of poetry with me, luckily including this one, so I feverishly looked up the poem: it was Ernest Dowson's '*Non Sum Qualis Eram Bonae Sub Regno Cynarae*', with its plaintive refrain:

And I was desolate and sick of an old passion . . .
I have been faithful to thee, Cynara! in my fashion.

I knew Leslie's fastidiousness in sexual matters too well to take the poem literally, but only as he intended that I should: that though he had met many other girls on his leaves in Alexandria and Cairo, he still cared only for me. He went on to say that he had heard from a mutual friend whom he had met in Alexandria that I had a good job, and added: 'Mother said, in an old letter which took months to reach me, that it was in the Foreign Office. I am so glad; it sounds pretty good to me, and makes me feel just a poor bloody soldier.'

I was flooded with joy, and all at once it seemed the most important thing in the world that he should know that I still loved him, too. It would be the most terrible calamity if he were to be killed not knowing! But I was stupidly shy of an outright avowal, and took refuge in adapting a phrase from the poem, saying that perhaps the 'pale lost lilies' were not lost after all. Of course I was in a fever to hear again, but as his regiment was sent back into the line, I did not have further word till April, when he responded to that phrase with the comment: 'I think you would consider that *this* lily has grown into rather a thistle . . . seriously, though, I'm not the same little lad you last saw; I *feel* so much older because of my life in the last year.' Then the letters came fairly regularly, but they were strange at first – sometimes almost assuming the old relationship, sometimes defensively impersonal, as if he were afraid – we both were – to take too much for granted. I am sure that if we could have met, all estrangement would have vanished instantly; but, having to rely on the written word (and that in the cramped space of air-letters which took so long to come and go), and missing expression of face and tone of voice, to which we were both very sensitive, we kept up our guard for a time.

Little by little I learned Leslie's recent military history. On leaving the Ayrshire Yeomanry and asking for a Middle East posting, he had sailed on the *Queen Mary* around the Cape of Good Hope and had docked at Durban. This was a city famed for its hospitality to servicemen. The citizens were literally waiting to seize the disembarking troops and bear them off to their homes for lavish entertainment, while singing on the quayside was the ample figure of Perla Siedle Gibson, 'The Lady in White'. Leslie had an aunt in Durban, but by great misfortune disembarkation was on this occasion not allowed, and he did not meet the relative who had last seen him as a little boy in Scotland.

His arrival in Egypt coincided with the great crisis of June and early July 1942, when morale among the Middle East forces was at its lowest after the long retreat from Gazala, and the fall of Tobruk. There was confusion in Cairo and Alexandria and, in the Western Desert, Auchinleck was desperately holding the Alamein Line. Leslie had little opportunity, and no inclination, to become associated with those glorious bands of Cairo irregulars, 'Groppi's Horse', or the 'Short Range Shepheard's Group'. He had been posted to the 11th Field Regiment, Royal Artillery, which was newly arrived in Egypt from Iraq, and was immediately sent to the front. This regiment of regular gunners was to serve successively with the 1st Armoured and 5th Indian Divisions before finding longer-term employment as one of the three regiments forming the field artillery of the celebrated 4th Indian Division.

When the Eighth Army turned and stood for what was to be the first battle of Alamein, a tiny force consisting of the 11th Field Regiment and a part of the Essex Regiment was rushed to the Ruweisat Ridge with orders to plug the vital gap between the South African positions on the coast and the New Zealanders on the edge of the Quattara Depression. It was to this much dive-bombed, shelled and strafed position – described as a forefinger poking into Rommel's midriff – that Leslie came, and where he remained throughout the summer and autumn, constantly in action. The Ridge was a favourite target for Stuka dive-bombers and was attacked several times each day. Upon this nucleus of troops, the reconstituted 5th Indian Division formed up to hold the infamous Ridge, which they did through Rommel's critical Alam Halfa offensive at the end of August.

The appalling hardship, primitive conditions, tremendous heat on the exposed rocky outcrop, and the omnipresent spice of danger which he encountered on his first experience of active service, appealed to the adventurous and the Spartan in Leslie, and salved the conscience that had irked him during his long training and frustrating inactivity at home. The tedium and discomfort of life which prevailed between moments of action and danger, and the feeling that they would never be strong enough in morale or *matériel* to take the offensive themselves, were dispelled when Montgomery took command of the Eighth Army later in the summer. In September Leslie's 5th Brigade found itself part of the 4th Indian Division, and it was with this famous fighting force that he was to spend about the next nine months. He was proud to serve with the magnificent troops of this Division – Rajputs, Baluchis, Punjabis and Gurkhas amongst others – and to belong to an army given new pride and confidence in itself by an inspiring leader. He was impressed by the way that this new spirit had filtered through all units, down even to the junior officers and other ranks, both British and Dominion. Montgomery's new style of leadership met with Leslie's wholehearted approval. 'Battles are won primarily in the hearts of men,' Monty was to write of Alamein 25 years on. 'Such men are educated; they can think; they can appreciate. They want to know what is going on, and what the general wants them to do, and why, and when; they want to see and decide in their own minds what sort of person he is. I have never believed in dealing with soldiers by a process of "remote control"; they are human beings, and their lives are precious.'

Leslie's first letter to me after our estrangement was written on 23 January 1943, the day Tripoli fell, and three months to the day after the second Battle of Alamein had begun. His division, having seen a great deal of dogged fighting on and around Ruweisat before the Alamein offensive, had been lightly engaged in the great action itself, though of course, their guns took part in the famous opening barrage. As the Indian Divisions' official history records the fact, the men of the 4th had, at Alamein, 'been something more than spectators and something less than participants in the main battle. Their task of containing their adversaries, without committing themselves to outright attack, had been well and truly done.' The 5th Brigade, which Leslie's regiment supported, moved slowly forward on the division's right. Then, as their contribution to 'Supercharge' – the culminating attack of the Alamein offensive – the Brigade was entrusted with the job of cutting a path through the enemy defences. The infantry was shielded by a moving barrage laid down by massed artillery, the first of a number of concentrated shoots in which Leslie participated in the North African campaign. To quote again from the official history:

> At 2.30 a.m. a concentration of 400 guns opened on a front of 800 yards, and the barrage began to march across the minefields and defences at a pace of 100 yards in three minutes. This devastating wedge of steel moved like a shield before the Essex and Rajputana Rifles. It poured down a cataract which cleansed the ground of every deadly device. One officer said that it was so precise that his men could have leaned against it; another, that his only casualties were those who followed the wall too closely and became queasy from the fumes of explosives. Lines of tracer shell marked the borders of the corridor which the guns cut . . . At 5 a.m. the barrage stood still for half an hour while the infantry mopped up and re-formed behind it. Then on it went inexorably for another 65 minutes . . . The kidney-shaped ridge was in our hands. The 5th Brigade had gone clean through the enemy lines to a depth of 8,000 yards. Then came thunder out of the east as rank after rank of tanks came roaring past, plunged through the infantry and turned north for the kill. The sun rose on the last of Alamein.

The 11th Field Regiment had supported the advance through the Western Desert, past all the names the Eighth Army knew so well in victory and in retreat, and now in victory again; through Egypt into Cyrenaica; and through Roman North Africa to El Agheila. Here on the border of Tripolitania Leslie's brigade had halted. 'We couldn't chase Jerry very well,' he wrote, 'as we were a trifle battle-scarred, so we were taken out. We did have hopes of being re-equipped for this Tripoli show,' – by coincidence he was writing on the very day Tripoli fell – 'but they didn't materialise, so we shall have to seek the bubble reputation elsewhere. Actually, we have earned our quiet time, for six months continuously in action is enough for anybody . . .'

A period of rather dull winter training in Cyrenaica ensued, but by the spring his battery, now detached from the rest of the regiment (which was in the rear, and which was later withdrawn to Egypt), was again in action. From Tripoli the advance into Tunisia involved him in some of the bitterest fighting of the war: in the Matmata Hills on the outflanking of the Mareth Line; at Wadi Akarit, where he had a narrow escape when he received (as he modestly put it, doubtless so as not to worry me unduly) 'a wallop from a piece of spent shell', but was not badly injured; and at the drive north to Enfidaville. The performance of the 4th Indian Division among the mountains of Tunisia was one of the high points of the North African campaign. Montgomery said that the spring offensive of 1943 was 'the heaviest and most savage fighting we have had since I have commanded the Eighth Army'. It was a source of great pride to Leslie that he was able to see this final phase of the war in Africa through to the very end. As well as the thrill of danger there was the considerable intellectual satisfaction of taking part in the very sophisticated artillery barrages on closely defined targets which distinguished the assistance the gunners gave to the gallant infantry in the struggle to break through the defences of Tunis; and his unit supported the epic fight of the Gurkhas, the Rajputana Rifles and the Essex Regiment on Garci.

It had been in Essex that, out of discontent with sitting at home, Leslie had requested a posting abroad; and it was somehow appropriate that it was with the men of Essex that he should have ended the North African campaign. But at Tunis his own career was once gain to take a new turn.

★ ★ ★

Now that I was in touch with Leslie again, I became very happy at Bletchley, in spite of anxiety over his safety. Wendy and I had decided that we did not want to remain in Wolverton, if we could go to one of the more interesting towns nearby. We were agreed that of all the billeting areas, Bedford would probably be our choice. It was a large town of some character, with a slow-moving sinuous river, aptly named the Great Ouse, meandering between bosky banks. The place had literary connections. John Bunyan, whose statue was prominent in the town, was born in the nearby village of Elstow. At Olney, not far away, William Cowper had written the *Olney Hymns* in collaboration with the former slave-trader John Newton. It was Newton, curate of the parish, who wrote the now hackneyed evangelical hymn 'Amazing Grace'. I was, moreover, amused by the juxtaposition of names in the Bedford High Street – Blood, Sand, DeAth: the bullring, of course! – which made me think back to my special subject paper in the finals, on the Spanish Background of English Literature. On such whimsical criteria, and perhaps thinking them a good omen, did we decide our preference. We realised, however, that the hard-pressed Billeting Office would be unwilling to countenance a move unless we went 'two into one'; but we did not mind at all the prospect of sharing.

I felt a little guilty at leaving the Websters, as we had developed quite a good relationship. Through them I first learned (as Leslie learned in the army) that bathrooms and books were not then things to be taken for granted – that reading was not an instinct like breathing and eating, but a skill sometimes painfully acquired. Mrs Webster had a Friend (to whom she always gave a metaphorical capital letter in speech), and she told me how much her Friend liked reading. She once asked my advice on a birthday gift, so I suggested a book. 'Oh,' said Mrs Webster, 'she *has* a book.' Books were not possessions to be accumulated and, in this town without a library, reading really meant newspapers and magazines. Mrs Webster was very understanding about my wanting to team up with Wendy, which was how I put it to her; and when I left she gave me a Victorian glass inkwell and a brown ironstone plate, because I 'liked old things'.

CHAPTER 10

A Woman . . . her name was Dull.
JOHN BUNYAN: *THE PILGRIM'S PROGRESS*

Ex Africa semper aliquid novi.
PLINY THE ELDER: *HISTORIA NATURALIS*

We arrived at our new lodging in Althorp Street, Bedford, feeling a little suspicious, as the Billeting Officer protested rather too much that the billetors were anxious to have us. The houses were even meaner than those in Wolverton, and much more dilapidated. As we went up the almost perpendicular staircase, Wendy pulled the banister away from the wall. Stifling a giggle, she hazarded a guess that the wardrobe would be full of the son's clothes. It was. There was nowhere for us to put our belongings. Our landlord, William Sugden, was a moulder in a metal foundry; he was also an ex-heavyweight boxing champion of Bedford, and had sadistic inclinations. His wife was large, vacant-faced and stupid. He told us what sport it was to take her to the 'Houtsize 'Ouse' in London, first putting her on the Circle Line, getting off smartly himself, and leaving her to go round and round until his amusement wore off. How he knew from which coach to retrieve her is a puzzle; I expect he was telling a tale, but even this made him a very disagreeable character. He used to come home smelling of iron-filings, and would sit down, unwashed, to a monstrous pile of chopped heart. Wendy and I felt our gorge rise, and simply could not eat. Poor Mrs Sugden considered we were being very superior and took offence. The only dish she made that we could tolerate was syrup tart, which we praised extravagantly, with the result that it became our unhealthy staple diet. Mrs Sugden meant no harm to anyone, but neither had she the intelligence to be really kind.

There was no atmosphere of narrow morality in the house — scarcely any evidence of mental activity at all, let alone a moral climate — but on the wall of the living-room was a pictorial chart of 'The Ascent to Heaven and the Descent to Hell', snakes-and-ladders style, and on either side of the entrance to the everlasting bonfire were the figures of Venus and Bacchus, the whole chart a vulgar allegory to set beside that Bedfordshire classic, *The Pilgrim's Progress*. When the question of bathing arose, there was always some difficulty. The statutory weekly bath was usually evaded, but about once a fortnight Mr Sugden grudgingly produced a papier-mâché moon-bath. This was placed on the kitchen floor, illiberally filled with water, and Wendy and I had to choose between going in together or one after the other while, we strongly suspected, Mr Sugden enjoyed a 'what-the-butler-saw' entertainment of looking through the keyhole.

I saved up these incidents to amuse Leslie in my letters, and related as much as I could about our domestic and leisure activities. I told him about the weekend we spent in Kent where Wendy's brother was stationed, and how we had visited Canterbury Cathedral on our way to Charing, which meant, I explained pedantically, a 'turn' on the Pilgrim Way. Leslie, however, could go one better: 'It must be nice,' he replied, in a piece of monumental understatement, contained in a letter written during a lull in the fighting at Wadi Akarit, 'to ramble round the Pilgrim Way. *This* way is not really exciting, but Belisarius fought here 1500 years ago, so we are in distinguished company . . . Life is very crude, and bonnie Princes Street a dream, but we soldier on with a good grace. Our Division has been mentioned in the news, and we've been patted on the head by Montgomery. Small things, perhaps — mere hot air — yet the lads are touchingly pleased to think they are appreciated.'

Some weeks later, after the fall of Tunis and the Axis surrender in French North Africa, when he had time to reflect on his past and present condition, he started to write more regularly. The letter-writing was beginning to lose its inhibition:

> The past year has been the most peculiar and the most
> testing in my life. There were many hours of boredom and

discouragement, even more of physical discomfort – the flies, the corpses stinking in the sun, dysentery, too, and hours of mental agony and nervous strain – those horrible Stukas last summer in Egypt. And sometimes there was the excitement of a good fight. Perhaps you think that the 'lust of battle' doesn't exist nowadays; believe me, it does, and it's an odd experience. Yet, when one looks back, it all seems dim and forgotten already, except for the silly little incidents which stick in one's mind, such as when we were dive-bombed one morning and the sergeant-major fell into his porridge! . . . It was a hot flame, but a clean one . . . Since I've been in the East, I've met many women – Egyptian, French, Greek, Jewish, Turkish and English, too. They had a certain similarity, all of them, and they all lacked something, though most were very beautiful to look at. *You* have that something.

★ ★ ★

Meanwhile, at Althorp Street, Mrs Sugden kept her wireless on loud and continuously, and on the morning of 10 July 1943, I heard from our bedroom some dramatic news. I rushed downstairs, and burst into the living-room: 'I hear we've invaded Sicily!' I exclaimed. 'Aoew,' she replied, 'I never listen to *them* things!' Yet she had a son stationed in the Isle of 'White' (as she pronounced it, and wrote on her letters to him), and another in the Home Guard; and our unwelcome presence was evidence enough that there was a war on. She was, however, bemused by the spate of air-letters arriving for me. When my cousin, who was to be in the locality (one did not ask why at that time, and it was only after we were both freed of our vows of secrecy more than 30 years later that he told me had been at Bletchley Park itself) suggested coming to visit me, Mrs Sugden had no doubt but that this was my 'gentleman friend'. No amount of denial and explanation would convince her otherwise. Even Mr Sugden made himself available to meet the visitor, ready to assume that here was the returning warrior, eager to see areas of the country which only *he* could recommend. 'You go to Berk'*am*stead,' he pronounced. 'That's the place. I know. I *been*.' Mr Sugden was, I think, a preliminary sketch for Alf Garnett.

We used to come home after evening shift, about 1.30 a.m., to find two sets of false teeth in tumblers on the living-room table. Wendy, whose sense of humour was more practical than mine, had the almost irrepressible desire to mix them up, but decency prevailed. We had a considerable degree of pity for Mrs Sugden, whose feeble-mindedness made her the butt of her husband's callous disposition.

My letters were now addressed not from the Middle East Forces, but from the British North African Forces and, moreover, headed 137/166 Newfoundland Regiment, R.A. This quite confused me for I had never heard of Canadians in North Africa – even though I knew that Newfoundland was not really Canada. Leslie's next letter offered some explanation of his position:

> Certain strange events have been taking place . . . culminating in the above address, and I was unable to write while wandering about Africa . . . I really didn't intend to join this regiment; in fact I was making efforts to rejoin the Yeomanry, who are out here [his former regiment had landed in Algeria as part of the 6th Armoured Division in the First Army and had supported the 1st Guards Brigade in the battle for Tunis], but the CO of this regiment chose me by interview and I had to go, being only a very small cog in the wheels of war. Frankly, I was quite pleased to leave the 11th, for all fighting was over, and a regular outfit is very boring and narrow-minded when not in action. I still don't like regulars any more than I ever did; the officers are not *too* bad, but the men are not a good type, and the ex-ranker officer is a strain to live with. These Newfoundland chaps are most likeable – Nature's children, woodsmen and fishermen, very tough physically, but not so 'smart-Alec' as the British soldier, and mostly of Scots and Irish descent. Most of the officers, who come from the British Army, are Scots, too . . . So I am now a 'colonial' and wear the badge of my adopted land on my shoulder, just like all the others.

As well as the few Canadian troops who were in fact sent to that theatre for training, this odd colonial unit also found itself there.

From his new campsite in Tunisia Leslie wrote:

Tonight we had a little concert from a first-class military band. The drum-major was terrific, with his jaunty swagger, and the lads loved it. So did I, to be truthful. I suppose I'm sentimental, but I defy anyone not to enjoy a little of the trappings of soldiering. If you had seen that band drawn up on the parade ground, with full regalia glittering in the sun, while in front six bugles sounded Retreat and the audience came spontaneously to attention, you'd have liked it, I'm sure. We get little enough music, and *no* glamour. Which brings me to a serious point, my dear. I think I can promise that life with me, whatever else it may be, will not be humdrum. Not that I mean it to be a breathless race, but rather that I somehow don't see life in an ordinary manner, not even this sere and monotonous existence in Africa; granted, it browns me off sometimes, but I do pretty well on the whole; and if I can still enjoy this incredibly austere and disciplined life, how much more shall we not enjoy life together? I say *we*, for I feel that you look on things in the same way . . . You'll see that I quite ignore the fact that in my 'austere' life, my daily menu would make you green with jealousy. Not that you and I ever worried about the fleshpots anyway, though we've probably both learned to appreciate them a little more than in the tranquil days before the war . . . Last night I was reading an article about wages, and I realised (with a *little* male surprise) that you must be earning about three times as much as I do. Still, I hope I've no false pride, and I'm very pleased.

It was clear to me from this letter that we were engaged again, if that was what I wanted, and I did; also, that the natural happiness and buoyancy of Leslie's nature had reasserted itself, now that it had been released from what he had felt to be the cramping frustration of home service. I wrote to the effect that I did indeed look forward to life with him, and that my guidelines for living were the same as his. Then the last barrier came down.

* * *

When our engagement was broken off, neither of us would take back the other's ring. I had given Leslie an antique bloodstone in quite a massive setting, with the motto *Spero Meliora* engraved on the seal.

> I never took off the signet [Leslie now wrote] and never would admit to myself why I didn't. But you know I always loved you, darling, and, being a mere male, didn't *have* to take it off. What false advantage we fellows have! . . . When I left home, I thought, in my pride, that I should be sufficient unto myself, like my friend the cat. But I very soon found that I was much more like the companionable dog! All through the African campaign I longed to hear from you, and found it hard at times to keep a stiff upper lip without your help. I would have written far sooner, only – to be quite frank – I feared a snub, and I don't think I could have borne it . . . I felt that you would not see why I had gone abroad. A good bit of it was selfish, but I also had the strange wish to see if I could 'take it', and to make my military service worthwhile. It's been an odd kind of fulfilment; and it has quite knocked on the head all the priggish ideas I may have had, and given me a sense of values. When I look back, I'm inclined to think that we were both, in some ways, a couple of prigs, and given to spiritual pride!

I had to agree with him. As a postscript, he added: 'Anyhow, we've both survived our own foolishness, and that's the main thing!'

I was overjoyed that our letters had regained their old intimacy, and I wrote telling him how much I delighted in sharing his thoughts once more. I was also secretly happy and secure because I knew he was out of the fighting. From his next communication I should have heard the warning note:

> My dear, my thoughts are not worth sharing just now. I have one of my pretty rare fits of *le cafard*, and I thought a letter to you would help. This really is the most wretched country you could imagine. With no prospect of campaigning, and stuck away in a bleak piece of desert, I find things get a bit

grim sometimes. Our only means of escape is alcohol, and I
keep off that pretty much; but I can't say I blame chaps for
getting drunk (apart from the fact that it doesn't do you any
good), for few of them take any interest in books. I've gone
through all our little library, and am now reading a
Galsworthy I found. But although I said I was reasonably
Spartan, this bare Nissen hut and my little windy bivouac
pall a bit at times. I'd give anything for a sight of you in your
pleasant civilian dress, and even the 'digs' would seem a
veritable palace compared with sand and ragged Arabs, and
khaki-drill shorts.

It was indeed true that many of the camps of the Eighth and First
Armies in French North Africa were unpleasant in the extreme; a war-
ravaged land in tropical summer heat, with all the squalor of
collapsing French colonial administration, disease and boredom.
Fortunately, there were opportunities for temporary escape. For the
next two letters told of an almost idyllic and peacetime existence. The
first suggested an atmosphere of schoolboy jollity:

The Mess is unwontedly quiet this Sunday morning; there
was a very big party last night at the Sergeants' Mess and all
the officers were there. 'Nuff said. But I have adopted the
French habit of diluting wine with water, and so I ate my
breakfast in solitary state this morning and regarded the
world with quite a sparkling eye. Which reminds me that
some bright sparks got the five ducks which our Mess has
acquired *very drunk* the other day by feeding them on a pap of
bread and over-ripe grapes. It was the funniest sight I've seen
for a long while, but hardly fair on the birds . . . The time I
like best is the evening when it's cool. I generally go off to
bed quite early, lie in my little bivouac, smoke a cigarette,
and think of you. You know, darling, I carry a very clear
picture of you in my head, and probably some of my
thoughts might make you feel shy – and glad, too, I hope!

The second letter came from a rest-camp by the sea where he had three days' leave and a chance for the first time in many months to reflect on life. We live in little beach chalets and look out all day on the Mediterranean; its blueness always surprises me, though I've seen it so often. My batman, who is a positive Jeeves, is with me and, truly, I am far less aware of being at war than I was in England. I bathe whenever I feel like it, drink iced wine on my verandah in the evening, and lead a dolce far niente existence. And yet, I'm restless, for we are definitely not going into any present campaign, and the future seems a little empty. If I must vegetate, I'd rather do so at home, in spite of the undoubtedly superior ménage here. I've got a streak of austerity somewhere!

This idleness in Tunisia after the campaign was over proved to be his fate. He obviously was of a mind with Churchill who later was to say: 'I never meant the Anglo-American Army to be stuck in North Africa. It is a springboard, not a sofa.'

Leslie took the opportunity to visit Carthage: 'There is literally nothing there,' he wrote, 'but I felt the atmosphere – or maybe I imagined I did.' It has often seemed to me that the combination of boredom after intense campaigning and the only alternative offered – luxurious idleness – was indeed reminiscent of what the censorious historians of the late Roman Republic saw as the existence which sapped the fibre of Hannibal's army when in winter quarters in Campania after Cannae. For a British army encamped on ancient Carthaginian ground, it was perhaps natural to enjoy without too many qualms some at least of the diversions which Livy suggested had got the better of the Carthaginians. The Ayrshire Yeomanry had nine months of enforced near-idleness in Tunisia during which they attempted to return to their sporting pursuits. Leslie had wanted to rejoin his old regiment, presumably in the belief that they would be going on to Sicily and Italy without too much delay. In the event, he had become a Newfoundlander; but in any case the Yeomanry's long sojourn in Tunisia would not have satisfied him. North Africa had brought out in him something of the stern Roman. His next letter produced this bombshell – something new out of Africa indeed: 'I've often wondered if I'd ever actually have to write this . . . I have transferred to the Parachute Regiment.'

The words cut me like a sword. In wounded puzzlement I had a sudden flashback to the time immediately after Dunkirk, when Leslie had referred to the projected formation of a parachute corps, and to service in it as 'absolute certain death' in a 'suicide squad'. Of course he was then a half-trained recruit, and now he was fully acquainted with danger and better able to assess it (or, perhaps, on the contrary, more apt to underrate it). Also, in June 1940 the concept of airborne forces was, as far as the British Army was concerned, at its very inception and had about it the fearfulness of the unknown. Since then it had been discovered that one could be a parachutist and live. The Parachute Regiment itself had been founded in August 1942. It was in French North Africa that British airborne troops had first been deployed on any scale, and Leslie would have heard of their exploits in seizing airfields and other strategic points in Algeria and Tunisia. The idea of literally dropping in on the enemy and catching them unawares would have seemed attractive after several months' idleness.

But the enigma of character was manifesting itself again, this time even more strongly and curiously. Joyfully and thankfully reconciled with me, and having proved himself in a very arduous campaign, he might well have rested on his laurels in comfort and safety, waiting for the war to end or to be drafted to some new theatre of operations. But some irresistible compulsion drove him on to hazard again the life he relished so much, and to put at risk my happiness as well. However, I had learned my lesson. I loved a man with *spirit*. That is how he was. As he had once said, he did not really have the temperament of a gunner. I had to accept the fact that he was an individualist, and that for him the only tolerable war was one in which he felt he was making some personal contribution – personal, but never 'glory-seeking', as he had made clear in 1940, not least by being prepared to postpone obtaining his commission. I think I knew in my heart that once again he wanted to do something 'useful, in the sense that it's got to be done'.

Thus, summoning all my courage and self-control (easier to do on paper), I replied wishing him luck, and sent by surface mail the photograph he had asked for. When this eventually reached him, he acknowledged it, saying:

The sea-mail letter arrived this afternoon, and my hands shook so much when I retired to my tent that I could hardly open it . . . For the photograph, God bless you. I just sat and looked and looked. Dear Irene, you are more beautiful than I remembered . . . There was a faint perfume, too, clinging to the photo, and it made me feel very homesick. My world of smells consists of things like bully-beef, unwashed humanity, and the stink of cordite. In towns, however, you do get the 'smell of the East', and it certainly is mysterious. I can't place what else there is except camel-dung. There's no doubt that while the East is fascinating in many ways, most people who write of it overlook its two outstanding features – sand and syphilis, especially the latter, which is very prevalent. The sand, in spite of storms, is queerly beautiful in its fashion, and the desert exerts its own influence on you. I liked it far better than *this* North Africa, which is more 'civilised' and cultivated.

He then made the following comments, from his own observations; it is the privilege of later generations to make a moral evaluation of a young man's opinions.

Discipline is 100 per cent tighter on foreign service; it has to be, for the British soldier is the most childlike creature, and the way that our 'coloured brethren' try to take a rise out of him is truly remarkable. Once I was prepared to give all these Eastern peoples fair judgment. But, with the exception of the Senussi Arabs, the people of the African littoral may be best described by the army slang 'wogs'. They are expert thieves, and by no means above murder. 'East is East' seems to be right. But *not* the Indians with whom I had year. They're magnificent, and if all their people were like them, I'd say Home Rule for India '*ek dum*'! But the Indian soldiers themselves are against it just now.

A few days later I received two letters. The first one mentioned again the photograph I had sent: 'I've almost gazed the gloss off the film by

this time! Seriously, though, it gives me a fresh pang every time I look
. . . Please could I have a lock of hair? I left the one I had in my old
Bible at home.' In the second letter, Leslie registered his thoughts
about the Italian surrender:

> Last night we celebrated the defeat of Italy – our brigadier
> ordered a rum ration to all ranks in honour of the occasion –
> yet I can't help feeling just a bit sorry for the Italians, and have
> never found it in my heart to dislike them as I do the
> Germans. The Italian prisoners have always been so pathetic.
> People laugh at them, but a dispirited army is a miserable
> spectacle; only their officers are despicable, for they treated
> their men like dirt, and reaped their harvest of desertions . . .
> Do you realise that I've been soldiering longer than anything
> else since I was a schoolboy? When I look back, I see how easy
> and comfortable and pleasant my life was, and I took it all for
> granted! I never thought I was soon to see just how miserable
> the peoples of the earth can make life for themselves. I didn't
> care two pins about killing Boche, but I did get upset at the
> spectacle of starving French civilians and Arabs when we first
> took Tunis. The whole irony of war lies in the fact that the
> persons who get hurt most are the inoffensive and the
> helpless.

★ ★ ★

Up till this time Wendy and I had endured the discomforts of Althorp
Street with cheerful good humour; but when we discovered *layers* of
stale milk on the saucepans, we felt we had had enough. We must look
for another billet. We knew that we should have to find this for
ourselves, as the Billeting Office would not be prepared to move us
again, nor lend a very sympathetic ear to our complaints. So, by dint
of various enquiries, we managed to locate a house in a more
salubrious area, Cardington Road, where the landlady was prepared to
offer us a small sitting-room in addition, for an extra guinea a week.
Even halved, this was a good deal to find out of our salaries. (I did not
earn, as Leslie imagined, three times his pay: in fact, I got £200 a year,

out of which I paid a pound a week income tax, a guinea a week for billeting, five shillings for transport, and the cost of meals at the cafeteria at Bletchley. Lacking travel warrants, I could not have come home on leave had my father not sent me the fare.) We reckoned, however, that the privacy would be worth the extravagance.

Highly delighted with the transaction, we made our way back to Althorp Street, wondering how we were to break the news to Mrs Sugden. As soon as we entered the house we heard a low moaning and, on opening the living-room door, saw our landlady rocking herself backwards and forwards in her chair. She looked up at us dolefully, and explained that she had 'fallen down in 'igh Street' and broken a bone in her foot. Consoling her was 'Sister Flo', emaciated and lugubrious, who had previously confided that she had 'been unfort'nate – I buried tew 'usbands'. Mr Sugden was at the pub, avoiding the necessity for sympathy. 'I'll 'av to tell yew girls to gaou,' wailed Mrs Sugden, and Wendy and I felt a frisson of mirth, quickly and ashamedly suppressed, at the way fate had played into our hands.

Poor Mrs Sugden had her leg put in plaster and was forced to bump herself down the stairs to get her husband's meals – he had no intention of spoiling her. The great and manly boxing champion stood and watched while we packed, roped and dragged our trunks down the narrow stair. Their son, who was in the Home Guard, called to visit his mother, and put his rifle through the cabinet of Gosse china. This was indeed the last straw: 'I never 'ad a bit o' luck,' said our landlady, 'since yew girls came into the 'ouse!' Such was our valediction.

* * *

At first our new billet appeared all that we could desire, and we revelled in the luxury of the sitting-room. Our landlady, a Mrs Brown, seemed pleasant and reasonable, and we were still contented to be in Bedford, although we had discovered that there was one disadvantage – the Americans. There were many US airbases in East Anglia and the Midlands, and the town was full of Yanks 'on the hunt'. Our pick-up point for transport to Bletchley was on the Embankment, near the Swan Hotel, and 'pick-up point' is just what the Americans thought it was! While we were waiting at about 10.30 p.m. to go on night shift, we were subjected to a certain amount of what would now be called 'sexual harassment', which we learned to parry quite neatly; but the arrangement did seem a little thoughtless on the part of the BP Transport Department.

As I have said before, the intellectual aristocracy of BP, who lived near the Park or had private transport, were able to take part in many home-made activities, such as the pleasure of organising and playing in small domestic chamber concerts, or chess, bridge, tennis, dancing and amateur dramatics. We lesser mortals who had been banished to such places as Wolverton were, however, less fortunate. The only public transport between Bletchley and Wolverton was the railway, and trains were infrequent. No recreation was arranged for those of us in outlying areas. There was, therefore, very little social *life*; I can write only of social *conditions*. There was no cinema, no dance-hall, not even a café, and as we had no centre in which to foregather (save The Galleon) and were all working on different shifts, it was impossible to take any initiative in organising group entertainment. I was billeted in Wolverton during the winter months, when the blackout was most restrictive. Indeed, apart from the occasional sortie to The Galleon, our chief diversion was to read – books brought from home, or bought in London or Oxford on a day off, as there was in Wolverton neither bookshop nor library. Even this pleasure was rendered impure, since, as we had no heating in our bedrooms, we were forced into the family sitting-room, and felt, out of courtesy, obliged to join from time to time in the general conversation – a pursuit not very rewarding to either party.

Now we were in Bedford, and it was summer; and the presence of these American servicemen certainly appeared to offer ample scope for amusement. We were, however, not encouraged to fraternise, as our establishment considered that the Yanks, being naïvely and pressingly inquisitive, and perhaps not possessing an inherited sense of the paramount importance of secrecy in wartime, might prove a security risk. And, well-indoctrinated also by the humorous posters of Fougasse, we were on our guard. On the Embankment they strolled along, surveying the local 'talent'. They were lonely, poor boys, like so many servicemen far from home, but their brash attentions grated and could be embarrassing: 'Hiya, babe! Say, don't you just look like

Veronica Lake! Hows about walkin' out with me?' I smiled and, deliberately misunderstanding, murmured some deprecating remark about having to catch my bus directly. Sometimes, waiting on the Embankment in the summer gloaming, one would become conscious of an approaching figure, and an arm would be slipped round one's waist, and a voice, in imitation of Bing Crosby, would croon, 'Moonlight becomes you, it goes with your hair', and then one had to move away, tactfully, but smartly.

I went once, with a friend, to a 'hop' in a church hall. I was wearing my engagement ring again, and I thought, innocently, that it would be protection from unwelcome advances. 'You engaged?' said an American soldier who asked me to dance. 'Where's your boyfriend?' 'In North Africa.' 'That's okay, then. How about you and me steppin' out? Gee, but you're cute. No kiddin'.' My natural reserve made me recoil at this blatant approach, as did my total commitment and loyalty to Leslie. But for girls who were unattached and less inhibited, and who yearned for a bit of 'fun', the prospect of lavish meals in American messes, and gifts of candy and nylons, accompanied, let it be said in all fairness, by flatteringly gallant, if brash, wooing, could be a powerful magnet. The honey-tongue (if not the fidelity) of the Polish officers was a legend, but the approach of some among their other ranks (even allowing for language difficulties) was even cruder than that of the US servicemen. 'You be my sweetheart – ten shillings?' was the invitation extended to one of my friends.

A booklet on instructions was issued to American servicemen landing in Britain, and in the light of today's freer manners, and of our familiarity with foreigners, the tone seems prim and earnest indeed: 'It isn't a good idea to say "bloody" in mixed company in Britain. It is one of their worst swear-words . . . To say "I look like a bum" is offensive to their [British] ears; to the British this means that you look like your own backside.' The GIs were advised also to 'spend money according to British standards', but this, naturally, they failed to do, as their ready cash was a large element of their success with local girls. Thus they caused deep resentment in the hearts of British troops, more taciturn, impoverished, and clothed in far rougher and less smart uniforms.

But if the company of the Yanks was 'out' for most of us, there were always the concerts in the Town Hall. Certain classical pieces came to symbolise the war – the Warsaw Concerto, for example, and, of course, Beethoven's Fifth Symphony, with its initial notes representing the 'V' sign in Morse. We all went often to the cinema; it was the great escape, and we drew comfort from, and identified with, films which ennobled or sentimentalised our situation – films such as *One of our Aircraft is Missing*, *The Way to the Stars* and *Mrs Miniver*. Enraptured by the celluloid screen, we revelled in the romance that had been denied to us, or had been put in cold storage 'for the duration'.

We listened to the wireless at every opportunity. As well as Churchill's leonine oratory, we enjoyed comedy programmes, such as Tommy Handley's *ITMA* which, if heard today, would seem childish indeed; but the programme was created for an age of less sophisticated humour, and depended upon topical references striking chords in the heart of a nation which was as one, and united in a common cause as never before or since.

The popular songs of the day encapsulated perfectly its mood – patriotism, courage, facile optimism masking anxiety and heartache: 'Coming in on a wing and a Prayer'; 'There'll Always be an England' (even the Scots seemed not to mind this!); 'We'll Meet Again' – all belted out with great fervour and sincerity in Vera Lynn's street-singer tones. Schmaltz, maybe; but we needed the sugar. Then at the height of the Desert War there was 'Lili Marlene', to which Marlene Dietrich's thrilling, husky, androgynous voice gave 'class'. This song appealed especially, as we had filched it from the Germans. So, similarly, in the First World War, we assumed proudly as an accolade of honour the Kaiser's ridicule of the first British Expeditionary Force as that 'contemptible little army'.

But suddenly, social life and entertainment, or the lack of it, faded into insignificance for me, with the arrival from North Africa of a mysterious and rather unsubtly coded letter which one did not have to be a cryptanalyst to interpret as evidence that Leslie was coming home. 'On receipt of this letter, don't write to me any more; it will be only a waste of time. Sorry to be so cryptic, and it's nothing to worry about – in fact, quite the reverse. I was never any good at poker, and I'm finding it difficult to write calmly to you. I can't tell you what's going on in my head. That's what they call discipline, I suppose.' I was mystified, and in a fever of expectation. Then on 1 November I received this telegram, with what I recognised as the consciously humorous overtones of 1914–18:

HELLO DARLING. BACK IN BLIGHTY. 14 DAYS LEAVE.
TRY JOIN. REPLY MY HOME. LOVE LESLIE.

I at once applied for leave, which was granted, and set off for Edinburgh on the overnight train. I got an affectionate send-off from my colleagues, along with much raillery and leg-pulling. I had expressed concern that after the long journey, probably spent standing in the corridor, I might look rather haggard, so the wearing of a yashmak was suggested, especially as Leslie would be used to seeing this item of female camouflage in the souks and cafés of North Africa from Alexandria to Algiers.

CHAPTER 11

The morning stars sang together.
THE BOOK OF JOB, 38. 7

As the train approached Edinburgh's Caledonian Station I found I was as nervous as on my first journey to Bletchley. What would Leslie be like? Would he be very much changed? What would he think of me? Would we feel easy together? To my shame, I even feared he might act the hardened campaigner – *miles gloriosus*. I had the advantage of seeing him first, eagerly scanning the carriages, and I observed that he was bronzed almost to the colour of teak. His face had lost its boyish roundness, and *there* was the debated moustache – I had always said I didn't fancy him with one – quite splendid, and at once my prejudice vanished. When we met I saw that his eyes were the same, soft and luminous; and there was no constraint between us.

We went straight to my home, and there, before my parents, Leslie pulled me on to his knee and said: 'Will you marry me?'

'I thought,' I replied lightly, 'that that was the idea!'

'I mean *now*.' I was dumbfounded. Our circumstances were unchanged. Leslie still had no degree, no money, no future prospects, and the war was far from over. But he felt he had proved himself a man, at 23, and, as the returning warrior, had a belief that there would be no parental opposition. There was none.

It was agreed that we should be married as soon as Leslie had completed his parachute training, which was the reason for his being sent home. He had to report to the Depot and School of the Airborne Forces, then occupying Hardwick Hall, near Chesterfield in Derbyshire. I, of course, had to return to Bletchley. But before we left we decided to spring a little surprise on two friends whose husbands were artillery officers in North Africa while Leslie was there. When I came home on leave I used to meet them in Crawford's Oak Hall in Princes Street, and now I made the usual arrangement. After we had greeted each other and ordered coffee, Leslie walked in. There was no home leave from overseas and, as far as I knew, few individuals or units of the Eighth Army had returned to Britain, for most had been sent to Sicily and thence to the toe and heel of Italy, or to Salerno, and by this time were fighting hard up the Italian peninsula on one or other side of the Appennines. And so the sight of this deeply sunburned soldier turned all heads. Leslie and I very much enjoyed the situation, though I felt just a little guilty at flaunting a privilege denied to my friends.

★ ★ ★

When I arrived back at BP it was to further billeting problems. Just when we thought we were comfortably settled, Mrs Brown informed us that some friends who took a stall in the Bedford market were coming the next Saturday and that, as she had always put them up, would we mind sleeping in the kitchen on a sofa and a shake-down? We were a little discomfited by the request, but agreed to accede to it this once; but when we realised that it was to be a regular arrangement, we knew that we should have to move again, for over and above the inconvenience of being put out of our room, we were sure that our landlady did not even change the sheets. But the greatest drawback was the impossibility, when on night duty, of sleeping by day in our landlady's busy kitchen. Leslie was disturbed to hear of this latest small trauma: 'It distresses me,' he wrote, 'to think of you being chivvied about in the way you are; after all, the army supports me, and when it moves me thinks a *wee* bit about me. And all places are alike to me, if you're not there – though, thank God, I'm no longer the cat who walks by himself!'

It had become clear to me that both Leslie and I had changed – not in essentials, but we had grown up. Leslie was happier than he had been since joining the army. He had proved himself in battle, he had been of service. I was happy because I was now 'on the inside', doing war work and feeling, for the first time, that we were really a partnership; and I was proud that I had grown more confident and mature enough to take Leslie as he was, and no longer demanded – as he had once said that I did – that he be the White Knight. I even felt that I was able to accept his new and perilous choice of military service.

We both recognised the change. From North Africa Leslie had written that he noticed an alteration in my handwriting, and teased me, saying that it was 'the fist of a determined woman'. And after we had met again, he observed that I had achieved what he called 'poise'.

> I want you to know and I think that you do – that I love you more than I ever did before, but in a slightly different way. I never stopped loving you, but somehow since I've been abroad, and you've been 'out in the world', we seem to have struck a deeper note, and more powerful . . .

The billeting problems seemed very minor compared to my happiness, but Wendy and I still had to find somewhere to live. We asked around, and eventually we had a tremendous stroke of luck. We joined up with three other girls in the Manor House at Old Wolverton. Here was a billet totally different from any we had experienced before. It made us feel as if we had progressed up the Bletchley ladder. Our new landlady made it clear that she was delighted to accept us in preference to yet more evacuee children. The parcel of land on which this house was built was mentioned in *Domesday Book*. As a parting pleasantry, I reported this to Mrs Brown, our Cardington Road billetor. 'Oh,' she replied, 'I must get it out of the library!'

We were back again in the Wolverton area, but now I did not care, and the house itself was luxurious compared with past billets. Wendy and I shared a room which was quite spacious, with pleasant furnishings. It was now November, and coming home in the blackout caused me a little nervous anxiety at first. There was a pond in the Manor House grounds, but even with my poor sense of direction, I soon learned to negotiate it, though I remained apprehensive of collision with the horses which roamed in the paddock.

The other residents were two friends, Marjorie and Heather, and a girl with the lyrical name of Charmian Romanis. We had our own kitchen/dining/sitting-room, and were to look after ourselves. We arranged that we should take turns to cook for whomsoever was on the same watch. Marjorie and Heather spent hours poring over cookery books, which seemed to me a strange occupation for Oxford graduates, especially in the face of wartime rationing; but perhaps it was a matter of the fox and the grapes, for I myself had not acquired any culinary skill. Indeed, my future mother-in-law defended me against criticism in this regard, with the quelling reply: 'She has a trained mind, and nothing to unlearn!' I was grateful for her championship and her charity.

Trained mind I might be supposed to have, but this did not stop me from losing my clothing coupons. This could not have come at a worse time, with the prospect in view of becoming an 'officer's lady'. I really would have to acquire a few pairs of stockings and dispense with my poodle anklets. I needed a new winter coat and did not have the skill that Wendy had to make one out of a blanket. It seems extraordinary now to look back and remember how we improvised as we did during the war. The idea of Wendy's tailoring enterprise in making a violently checked blanket-coat puts one in mind of escape committees in German POW camps making enemy uniforms out of British battle-dress or bedding. In order to have my clothing coupons replaced I had to be vouched for by a responsible person, and Leslie's uncle, who was a KC and Sheriff-Substitute of Fife and Kinross, kindly did this for me. These safeguards were important. One of the girls in Hut 6 at Bletchley lost her food ration book. She had it replaced, and when the old one turned up she was tempted by hunger into using both. This was a serious offence, and she was dismissed. But this in itself must have been a difficult decision for the authorities: to dismiss her was to create a security risk and, as she had proved herself dishonest, to retain her was also a potential threat to Ultra.

The arrangements for our wedding were being handled admirably by our families. There were complications on account of our both being (in that pleasing Scottish legal phrase) 'furth of Scotland', and the difficulty of fixing a date because of our respective duties. 'In a glorious letter from Mother,' Leslie wrote, 'she waxes indignant about the formalities we must satisfy, and says that getting married seems to be in the category of committing a crime.' With affectionate humour he described her and his favourite aunt as being like 'a couple of Bengal matches – you know, those fizzy things with a pink light'. An important factor, too, was the change of name on my ration book. The new book was to be handed to me by the minister, the Revd Dr Adam Burnet, only after we had signed the register – no self-respecting hotel would have accepted us with different names.

But the date remained the real problem. Leslie had first to undergo a stiff PT course at Hardwick, but he found to his relief that he had not deteriorated from the peak physical condition which, despite those months of idleness, had achieved for him in North Africa his acceptance into the Parachute Regiment. 'You'll be amused to hear that I'm very stiff and sore. I've carried weights, swung on beams and parallel bars, jumped ditches, scrambled over walls, scaled rather terrifying cliffs by rope, and generally behaved in the fashion of an anthropoid ape. And my hands are rather cut about, but I'm still cheerful.' A few days later he confided:

> The most back-breaking part is over, thank goodness . . .
> Today we had one of those famous assault courses, followed
> by a ten-mile forced march; my platoon did it in one hour and
> forty minutes, which is not too bad. But if you could see me,
> you'd think me but a sorry object to hobble to an altar. And
> not a thing of beauty, but rather like an ex-pugilist. Ringway
> [the airfield near Manchester where the actual parachute-
> jumping was undertaken] is still uncertain. We should have
> gone there this coming Saturday, but may be as much as a
> week late. Sorry to be so vague, darling, but blame it on the
> unreliable British climate. And if we are delayed a week, that
> means a lot of gratis PT and a battle course, which is not a
> pleasing prospect . . . Darling, they were playing 'One Fine
> Day' on the wireless a little while ago. It always gives me a
> twist inside to hear it. I remember listening to it once just
> before the Alamein battle. I felt so wretched, because I
> thought I might never see you again. You can be sure I count
> my blessings nowadays. It's almost a blessing to be bashed
> about.

Hearing of this preliminary training for the Parachute Regiment at Hardwick made me think up an indelicate version of the famous old rhyme about that prodigy house, 'Hardwick Hall, more glass than wall': 'Hardwick Hall, sore a–e when fall'. In the condition in which he so often found himself, this jingle amused Leslie quite a bit.

Having left the house of the famous Bess of Hardwick, he went on to the care of yet another Bess. The course at No. 1 Parachute Training School at Ringway involved a period of initial practice on a variety of ground-training apparatus. Recruits had to learn how to fall and land safely, and this they did from a variety of heights and by means of different contraptions. There was drill to teach the men to extricate themselves from the several hazards that might be encountered, for the dangers of a night drop over woods or water were obvious. Thereafter progress was to a real parachute descent. This was made from a tethered barrage-balloon, with a jumping-cage suspended below it. For the second time in his military career Leslie now encountered a piece of equipment to which an unattractive female name and personality was attributed. 'Auld Bella', the rudimentary gun at Harrogate, was replaced in his affections by 'Bessie' the captive balloon. From Bessie, and later from aircraft, a total of seven jumps by night and by day had to be completed before wings were awarded.

It was now December and the weather would not co-operate; day after day the fog came down. Of course I could not apply for leave until I knew when Leslie would get his. Several writers have emphasised the very stressful nature of the parachute training at Ringway. Cocooned in happiness, Leslie seemed to take it in his stride, his attitude one of cheerful impatience. The only hint at the effects of nervous strain came in a ribald verse current among the trainees, which he quoted to me:

> Jumping through the hole,
> Jumping through the hole,
> We always keep our trousers clean
> When jumping through the hole!

We had hoped to be married in the middle of December, but in the first week of that month, Leslie wrote: 'Can you stand by to shift the date to, say, 22nd December? Don't give up hope yet; after all, the delay may mean all the difference between a wedding – or a funeral! Not quite that, darling, but reasonable weather means a whole bridegroom at least.' Several days later he still could not name the day:

> I shan't draw breath or stop fidgeting until we're on that train to Glenfarg . . . I shall be tremendously relieved when the course is over. Normally, I wouldn't care two hoots, but having come home unexpectedly, and with the thought of our marriage dazzling me, I'm so happy that I keep expecting some obstacle to turn up. All of which goes to show that masculine reason and logic are perhaps not so strong as you may have supposed. Don't think that because I'm learning an absorbing and rather difficult trade I have no thoughts to spare for you. Quite the opposite; I think of you more than ever and make mental clutches at you like a frightened baby. *Never* have I known time to pass so slowly!

Leslie was awarded his parachute wings on 22 December. However, luck was not with us for, as a reward for jumping in the intervals of appalling freezing fog, he got flu as a Christmas present and was delayed for a few days in hospital at Ringway. But otherwise he had escaped unscathed. Hitting one's nose or forehead on the opposite side of the jumping-hole of the balloon or aircraft was called 'ringing the bell'. Leslie had clearly avoided this mishap, for the face that presented itself at the church to the sound of other bells was unblemished – only so very much older than that of the newly commissioned boy of the Stirling studio photograph, taken but three years before.

CHAPTER 12

My candle burns at both ends.
It will not last the night.
But, oh my friends, and ah my foes,
It makes a lovely light.
  EDNA ST VINCENT MILLAY: *POEMS* (1923)

We were married eventually on 29 December in St Cuthbert's Church, Edinburgh, in the little chapel which was a memorial to the fallen of the First World War. I wore a borrowed dress, and carried a huge, ungainly bouquet of chrysanthemums (in wartime there were no roses in December). Because of the difficulty in fixing a date, and as it was the Christmas season, it had been almost impossible to arrange a decent reception. In the end we had to settle for a hurried and depressing buffet in the North British Hotel, with a menu which would not have been out of place at a Sunday-school picnic. After an extremely modest amount of alcohol available for the toasts, the delighted guests had to make do with 'Lemonade/Orangeade'.

We were to spend our honeymoon in a rather dingy hotel at Glenfarg in Perthshire. None of this mattered, however, compared with the joyous prospect of being together. Anticipating the harsh lighting in our room, Leslie had brought with him some candles, and I was touched by the romantic tenderness of the gesture. We walked in the wintry Perthshire countryside and were happy and at peace, refusing to think beyond the present. There were two elderly ladies in the hotel – the only guests beyond ourselves – no doubt escaping the prospect of a lonely festive season at home. Clearly they recognised us as honeymooners, and were coyly sweet to us. We decided to go to a Hogmanay dance in the village hall, and they came along to watch. I still have the crudely duplicated tickets for this hop, amusingly priced in those days before sex discrimination was questioned, 'Ladies – 1/6'; 'Gents – 2/6'. It was not common at that time to see a soldier at home in Britain wearing parachute wings, for despite the Parachute Regiment – a newcomer to the army's Order of Battle – having mounted raids in France and Italy, and having taken part, with heavy casualties, in the Tunisian and Sicilian campaigns, airborne forces did not have a very noticeable public profile before the days of Normandy and Arnhem. Leslie's maroon beret and the winged flash on his shoulder attracted attention as we entered the hall. I was so proud of him, and maybe he preened himself a little, too!

Coming on leave first, I was first to return. Leslie followed me south, to report at the Airborne Forces Holding Unit at Clay Cross. I was welcomed back to BP with much good-humoured teasing. The wedding photographs, with Leslie in Ayrshire Yeomanry service dress, complete with breeches, boots and spurs *and* parachute wings, caused considerable amusement. What was he – Bellerophon? (In fact, with so many changes of unit, no military tailor could keep up with him, and he had felt that his old Ayrshire Yeomanry full uniform was the smartest kit for the occasion.)

After our return to duty I received a letter from Leslie:

> Somehow I feel a subtle change within myself since our wedding. I feel that our love has grown stronger, and I know that I miss you, darling, even more than before, for I really need you, as I expect you divined long ago. In some ways I am self-sufficient, and I try to be always self-disciplined. Briefly, it's that Spartan streak which I've spoken of before . . . but I need you, darling, both physically and spiritually, and particularly the latter, though they're both mixed up. I'm afraid I can't subscribe to the theory that man should always be 'bloody, bold and resolute'; but rather, I confess, that it's very comforting to lean on *you* sometimes . . . more especially as I've a funny instinct that if I follow your ways I can't go wrong, whereas my own existence is apt to be hardening, as you can see that it must be. My dearest love, I chatter about all sorts of odd news, when I really only want to tell you that my real self is in your keeping. I lead a reasonable existence with cheerful and friendly companions, but I always have the feeling that it isn't *real* and doesn't *matter*,

although I'm very aware of everything around me. We're both very conscious of our independent lives, and yet only feel truly alive when we are together. I used to think it bad enough parting from you, but now I feel it a hundred times worse. Oh, my love, after the war, wherever we roam, we'll be together and, no matter where it is, I shan't mind a bit, because you spell home to me.

In his next letter Leslie told me that on that day he had been assigned 'a rather painful duty . . . from 4 o'clock this afternoon for 24 hours I am escort to an officer under close arrest, a captain, I believe. This means sleeping in his room and hopping out for walks with him when nobody is about.' The following day he reported:

> The officer I have been escorting is a most pleasant chap, and I have really had a day's holiday. Yesterday evening we walked two miles through the snow to a very secluded little inn, which was a charming place – low rafters and a log fire. Mine host was the spit of John Bull, complete with corduroy breeches, check waistcoat, and a face like a cask of port. We played dominoes with an old boy and his wife; she was eighty, and if you'd seen her puffing cigarettes and drinking strong ale, you'd have been as dumbfounded as I was. Then two miles back to bed; an evening walk does this poor chap good (not me, the other!) and makes him sleep. This morning we slipped into Mansfield for coffee and a haircut; and now I'm just waiting to be relieved, and rush to the letter rack. I keep as many of your letters as I can store to look back on at the turn of the century, which we're both going to see!

Leslie was able to come to Wolverton Manor once or twice, and Wendy accommodatingly moved in with Charmian. Wires announcing that he had some leave would be sent to the delightful telegraphic address of BP which was 'Bonzo'. Only once did we have leave together for more than 48 hours back in Edinburgh. Having acquired a wife, Leslie began to think that he ought to take some steps towards securing our future. He did not feel that he would want to return to university, so he decided to apply for an unclassed 'War Honours' degree – 'probably not worth the paper it's written on', but perhaps enough to get him started in some profession, such as colonial service or, possibly, journalism; he rather liked the idea of becoming a parliamentary correspondent for a newspaper. He had not quite completed the required three years out of four, but his examination results had been good, so the Senatus stretched a point, and we both got leave to come to Edinburgh for the January 1944 graduation. It was a happy little celebration, and I thought the scholar-soldier, gown and hood over Sam Browne and tunic, with the ribbon of the Africa Star, looked very dashing indeed.

Some time during the few days' leave, when talking about my life – not work, of course – at Bletchley, I must rashly have let slip the fact that occasionally I was tired. We all were after a 'short change' (a shift from 4 p.m. till midnight followed by one from 9 a.m. till 4 p.m., all times excluding our transport). This seemed to upset Leslie disproportionately. I misunderstood the cause of his mood and remarked on it in a letter. I received the following reply:

> Here I am sitting on my little iron cot and feeling very lost without you, seasoned trooper though I may be. All the way down in the train I kept seeing you smiling at me – oh, so wistfully. Then when I reached the Mess, your letter was waiting for me, and it made me happy and sad at once, and I just HAD to write you a note, though I can't post it tonight. Darling – and I'm sure this won't be inopportune – don't worry about me, because I'm really quite a 'happy warrior'; it was the thought of leaving you, and the fact that you were going back to a hard grind, which prompted my outpourings. They can do what they like to me, but I hate the idea of your being messed about . . . I'm even more excited to get a letter nowadays than in the days when we were very young. I often think back on those days; they seemed so halcyon, but I don't regret their passing, for the days are now sweeter, even if so many must be spent apart.

Halcyon days they seemed to me now, for Leslie was within reach, and was not in action. *Never* since the war began had I been so happy. I shut out all thought of what was to come. But the bright eyes of danger beckoned again, and sooner than I had expected. Leslie told me that he was considering a further transfer to the Special Air Service.

CHAPTER 13

Who is the happy warrior? Who is he
That every man in arms should wish to be?
WORDSWORTH: 'CHARACTER OF THE HAPPY WARRIOR'

The Special Air Service Regiment – or SAS, as it soon came to be called – was at this time an established part of the Army Air Corps, though it was little known to the public at large. It had been founded as an irregular unit for service in the Western Desert by Colonel David Stirling, then a subaltern in the Scots Guards. Its purpose was to perform acts of sabotage and to organise raids far behind the enemy lines, and (later, in Europe) to sustain local guerrilla groups, and send back to Britain intelligence regarding any situation with which SAS troops themselves were incapable of dealing in the small numbers in which they operated.

Officers and men were all volunteers. Originally they had to drop a rank for the privilege of joining. Parachuting was only one of the qualifications for membership. According to Major-General John Strawson's *A History of the SAS Regiment*, its soldiers had to get themselves to the target 'by any means from submarine to caique'. Though they had to be 100 per cent fit, and the training was gruelling, officers and men were chosen not just for their brawn but for their intelligence, integrity, self-reliance and self-discipline. The contemporary 'macho' image which press and public have given to the regiment since they became dramatically aware of it during the siege in 1980 of the Iranian Embassy in London, is a false representation of what it was during the Second World War. Then it was a different sort of regiment because it was dealing with a different sort of enemy. Now, sadly (if the press is to be believed), they seem principally an anti-terrorist force, and whereas in 1944 their aims were sabotage and hitting a recognised enemy as hard as they could, today they are forced to deal largely with the un-uniformed enemy in our midst. In wartime they knew their foe – except when treachery intervened, as in Operation Loyton, east of the Vosges Ridge, where German sympathisers informed on them.

David Stirling stipulated the 'discipline, cleanliness, turnout and behaviour' must be as high as in the Brigade of Guards. There was to be no 'acting tough or noisy ill-discipline'; toughness was to be reserved for the enemy. 'Humility and honour' were essential requirements, and Stirling declared that 'the SAS brooks no sense of class . . . the idea of a crack regiment is one officered by aristocracy . . . in the SAS we share with the Brigade of Guards a deep respect for quality, but we have an entirely different outlook. We believe, as did the Ancient Greeks who originated the word "aristocracy", that every man with the right attitude and talents, regardless of birth or riches, has a capacity of reaching . . . that status in its true sense.'

The regiment worked in four-man modules, each man having a special skill (i.e. explosives or navigation), and officers and men had the same training, so that in the event of casualties they could be virtually interchangeable. According to Stirling, this led to a 'peculiar mutual respect and real friendship, a rare blend of the individual and the team'. General Strawson emphasises that 'absolute secrecy was not merely necessary in order not to compromise the success of operations. It was a kind of obligation to those organisations such as Ultra and other secret sources which supplied the highly sensitive and closely guarded intelligence required for an operation by the SAS to be mounted at all.' I find it a sad small dramatic irony that Leslie never knew what I did at Bletchley, let alone its significance in his own military enterprises.

Field Marshal Lord Wavell was strong in his support for the SAS. He had commented that one should never allow oneself to be 'trammelled by the bonds of orthodoxy'. It was this very quality of non-conformity for which Leslie had expressed admiration in June 1941 when Wavell was relieved of his Middle East command. At this same time Leslie had voiced his discontent at the 'ponderous inefficiency' and 'heartless bureaucracy' of the conventional army, and it was then that the ideas in Tom Wintringham's *New Ways of War* began to influence his thinking.

Of course this new venture was like a dagger at my heart. Indeed, a winged dagger was the SAS badge, originally conceived, it is said, as the sword of Damocles. Leslie reckoned that he would be in no more danger in the SAS than in the Parachute Regiment: or so he persuaded himself. He believed, without conceit, that not everyone could do this job and, as he felt that *he* could, it was up to him to do it. When Malcolm James's book *Born of the Desert* – the reminiscences of a doctor with the 1st SAS in the Western Desert – appeared in 1945, a reviewer wrote: 'All men have conscience, but it is given to only a few to have the selflessness to stride out into battle and, by themselves undertaking the combat that has to be done by *someone*, to satisfy its insistence . . .' Leslie was in a rapture of courage to play his part in finishing the war. The character-enigma was manifesting itself again. Newly married and ecstatically happy, he yet felt compelled to offer himself for one of the war's most hazardous enterprises. Two years previously he had wanted to hit back at fate for the death of his three cousins; now he was so joyful that he felt he must compensate in this sacrificial way. There was also, it has to be admitted, the continuing thread of excitement. His zest for living had to encompass even the risk of dying.

I believe I could have stopped him. When he joined the Parachute Regiment he was in Tunisia, and discussion was impossible. Now he was in Britain, within reach, and we could talk together. Also, we were closer than we had ever been. But I did not attempt to stop him. I was trying desperately to be unselfish, to let him make his own decision, to be himself. Perhaps, paradoxically, I was also acting the coward. I remembered so painfully the anguish of estrangement, and I felt I could not take the risk of spoiling our amity, nor of living with memories of discord, should he be killed. After all, I told myself, he might not be any safer in the Parachute Regiment than in the SAS. And so, together, we sealed his fate.

* * *

Having reconciled myself to the situation, I felt I had to make a gift to

Leslie of my acceptance. I turned to a medium natural to me when dealing with emotional occasions – versifying. I wrote for him the following poem; it seems to me now rather jejune, but it was the spontaneous overflow from a heart both proud and anxious, and not greatly concerned with turning out a literary exemplar:

Parachutists
(for L.G.C.)

See how the quiet shell of sky
Spills wind-looped lilies languidly;
And roses bursting in white foam
Curdle the still, blue heavenly loam.
Strange opiate dream! for these are men –
Winged with all cunning in man's ken;
Girt with dear courage not to yield,
And laughter, like a supple shield.
Look how they take their downward flight
In metaphysical delight!
They, Perseus-like, are pledged to slay
The Gorgon of our modern day,
And pay the monstrous debt of pain,
But half-discharged at Alamein.

★ ★ ★

In 1944 a Special Air Service Brigade had been formed in Ayrshire. The 1st SAS Regiment was at Darvel, the 2nd near Prestwick, and at Galston were the 3rd, 4th and 5th. The 3rd and 4th were French parachute battalions and the 5th a Belgian parachute company. The rugged countryside of Ayrshire had been chosen as that most nearly approximating to the anticipated terrain of the regiment's operations in France.

The 1st SAS had been reorganised, had accepted new members, and was to remain training at Darvel. I was consequently faced with a dilemma. If I stayed on at Bletchley – which I was reluctant to leave – I should scarcely ever see Leslie before the invasion of France, which we all knew was expected within a very few months. Officially, no one was permitted to resign from BP; we were presumed to know too much. As Peter Calvocoressi put it: 'Once in, never out.' But then, for women there had to be some exceptions – if one became pregnant, for instance. (This was a situation we had to avoid at all costs. My mother-in-law helped to run one of the early family planning clinics, and I had been despatched to an appointment with the other doctor!) There was one other condition of release: having a husband in the Home Forces who wanted his wife to be with him – a sop to the services, this. Leslie's commanding officer, Lieut-Col Blair (Paddy) Mayne, would not countenance camp-following wives, considering them too much of a distraction from the very intensive training which the regiment had to undergo. I reckoned, however, that if I went back to Edinburgh, I could see Leslie for the occasional '48 hours'. He would not put any pressure on me. I was to have my freedom of choice, too. But, sad as I was to leave the arena of Ultra, for me there *was* no choice. So I applied for my discharge and it was granted. I came home towards the end of March 1944, in time for Leslie's twenty-fourth birthday, though we were not able to spend it together. He had been born on Easter Day, surely the most hopeful date in all the year.

I had gone to Bletchley in excitement and trepidation, had been very content there, in congenial company, and with the satisfaction of knowing that I was employed on work essential to the war effort. But now, in the circumstances, I left without any heartsearching or serious regret.

★ ★ ★

The SAS was a happy outfit. The Very Revd Dr J. Fraser McLuskey, MC, who served as chaplain to the 1st Regiment, summed up its quality in his book *Parachute Padre*: 'It doesn't take long to sense the atmosphere of a strange Mess. In some the stranger is simply frozen. In this particular Mess I had hardly sat down before I felt completely at home, and before I had finished the meal, I had made up my mind that if this particular unit would have me, this was where I would stay. I found myself sitting between two young officers, both of whom I quickly came to know well. One was a fellow Scot, Leslie Cairns, and the other a Devon man, Roy Bradford. Before many weeks had passed we were to lose them both . . .' Later in his book, Dr McLuskey described Leslie as 'one of the finest officers and finest men in the regiment'.

In Paddy Mayne the regiment had an awe-inspiring commanding officer. An enigmatic amalgam of cold ruthlessness and surprising kindness and sensitivity, he was capable of striking terror equally into the enemy and any of his own side whom he considered too timidly orthodox. By early in 1944 he had already won the DSO in Libya, and a bar to it in Sicily. In a remarkable record, he was to go on to win two further bars, in France that year and in Germany in 1945. Leslie's squadron commander, Bill Fraser, and his troop commander, Alex Muirhead, were both Scotsmen. Fraser, originally a Gordon Highlander who had fought in France in the rearguard actions of 1940, had been in the SAS from the beginning, and both were veterans of classic raids in Sicily and Italy. I also remember meeting Johnnie Cooper, then a subaltern, but a long-serving ex-NCO who had been probably the first man recruited to the infant regiment by David Stirling. Today, when entering the Royal Academy at Burlington House, Piccadilly, whose who notice the Artists' Rifles memorial with SAS wreaths upon it, may wonder at the connection between 'Mars and Minerva'. This may be only a post-war Territorial Army link, but in 1944 at Darvel there could be found Major Ian Fenwick of 'D' Squadron. Fenwick, killed on Operation Gain near Fontainebleau in August, was a well-known artist whose delightfully humorous drawings illustrated *Songs of a Sub-Man*, by Patrick Barrington, whom we have already met as one of Bletchley Park's strange collection of eccentrics.

★ ★ ★

The terrain around Darvel in which the SAS was preparing itself was grim and hostile. Captain Derrick Harrison has described some aspects of the training:

> After dark, working by compass, we headed into the desolate
> Scottish countryside, our rucksacks weighted with filled

sandbags to get us used to travelling long arduous miles with heavy loads. With small token charges of explosives in our pockets we made for distant roads, railways and bridges, sinking up to our knees in bogs and wading through the icy waters of fast-running burns. In the dark hours before dawn we crept up on our objectives and laid charges. Sleepy Scottish hamlets awoke to the sound of explosives. We melted away again into the mists and learned to make our way back with unerring accuracy to places that were little more than pinpoints on the map.

The biographers of Paddy Mayne quote a veteran of the North African campaign: 'We thought it was tough dealing with extremes of heat. It was a treat compared with these bloody windswept moors, the biting wind and fog!'

None of this damped Leslie's spirits. He wrote light-heartedly of one of his own orienteering exercises: 'Tonight we have a pretty tough scheme, lasting from 9 o'clock till 7 tomorrow morning. It is an approach march of over 30 miles across some terrible moors, and the objective for my little band of happy warriors is two (large) bottles of beer! Do I hear a murmur about needles and haystacks? We get the morning off after the scheme, but I reckon we shall be pretty tired. Some people are jumping tomorrow, but they are those who have not done a jump for a long time; I expect I shall do another before leave comes off.'

In another letter he describes a further scheme:

> The march was longer than I expected and we staggered in at half past six this morning, having done 27 miles in just over nine hours, which isn't bad. I've never seen such terrible country; it was a constant stumble over grassy hummocks and peat-bogs. I was completely sunk to the knees and had to be pulled out with a squelch. Then I fell and banged my knee-cap on a stone and it's pretty stiff now. Even my lads, tough though they are, felt it hard, and only four of us finished out of seven. The others dropped on the moor, and lay there till dawn and then made their way home . . . It's the thought of

you that keeps me going when I begin to flag or feel a bit faint-hearted . . . Dearest love, I *do* understand how we are both merry on our all-too-short leaves. One has to be, but it doesn't blind me to the fact that we are both solemn underneath the surface. I think you are especially wonderful, the way you are so understanding about my odd career. I know that you worry, even though I beg you not to, and I love you all the more for being so sweet about it. I get a bit frightened myself sometimes – we all do, as no doubt you realise; but you help an awful lot to restore my courage. I don't envy other people their easier lives – too much comfort brings sloth! But I think we might have a little time to ourselves now, and be d—d to anyone who says we haven't both earned it!

Leslie's letters to me (perhaps on purpose) told only of the prankish, rollicking aspects of his experiences. He mentioned the 'war games': such as the capturing of a fire-engine; the cutting of telephone wires; the jape of climbing unseen into a baker's van and reconnoitering the town as the baker innocently made his rounds; and penetrating the docks and going to sleep on a submarine. Though all these exploits were undertaken with schoolboy high spirits, no one lost sight of the fact that these swashbuckling deeds of derring-do were a dress rehearsal for the serious havoc the men were to wreak in France.

The atmosphere of Darvel was well encapsulated in a verse of doggerel which Leslie added at the top of one of his letters:

> They seek us here, they seek us there,
> We always catch them unaware,
> And where *we* are they never guess,
> The d—d elusive SAS.

In spite of being a member of this élite fighting unit, learning to kill people in extremely unpleasant ways, Leslie retained the gentility of Victorian ellipsis in the matter of writing profanities!

On one exercise, clearly when the weather was no longer a hazard, Leslie wrote a 'diary' which made the training seem like a camping holiday:

11th May. My heart is so full of you, I must pour it out somehow, and so I've devised this little diary of my travels, and will write a piece each day. All day since dawn we have been lying on a soft bed of bluebells in a wood beside a river. I wish you were here, my dearest love; I know you'd like it. My sleeping-bag would hold two – like the one in *For Whom the Bell Tolls*. That book seems enormously appropriate in these surroundings. *He* did this sort of job, too, and if you were with me everything would be perfect.

12th May. My day has been spent in sleeping, reading a little, which at once made me think of you – and then, mostly, thinking of you, and feeling you so close . . . I have a French sergeant with me – quite a nice fellow . . . And now I must pack up and take the road; you'll be keeping me company on a long night march, although I know you're asleep in our nice warm bed . . . The War Office has raised you to the status of a 4/- wife [the daily allowance]; what fun, darling!

13th May. A very tough night march. We were all absolutely fagged out, and promptly dropped off to sleep at 4 a.m., only to be caught later by some children who betrayed us to the patrols. I was rather surprised, never having realised what a source of danger children can be.

All soldiers liked to feel they were appreciated, and a visit of inspection without 'bull' attached to it was welcome. Leslie reported one such descent on their camp: 'This morning we had a visit from "Boy" Browning [GOC, 1st Airborne Corps], who gave us a truly excellent talk, and then stayed to lunch. He is a most inspiring chap, obviously one of the Montgomery school, but toned down by his service with the Guards.'

★ ★ ★

Meanwhile, I had joined the Home Civil Service in the Department of Agriculture for Scotland at St Andrew's House. I was appointed to the

Land Utilisation Branch. The work involved the evaluation of land for the rival purposes of agriculture, housing, airfields, hydro-electric schemes, etc., and often resulted in acrimonious tussles between Agriculture and the Home and Health Departments. This was all very necessary, but I found it dull stuff indeed after the immediacy of Ultra.

I had been at St Andrew's House barely a week when a telegram arrived at my parents' home:

> MEET ME NORTH BRITISH GLASGOW 1900 HOURS
> TUESDAY. BRING BELT. LOVE LESLIE.

This referred to the cartridge-belt Leslie was having specially made at Anderson's of Edinburgh. My stomach lurched. This was IT. When we met, Leslie told me he had gone 'AWOL' to say goodbye. There was to be no embarkation leave, of course, because of the obvious necessity of preserving secrecy about the date of the invasion of north-west Europe. He told me he was about to go into a 'sealed camp' somewhere in the south of England, and that the letters he wrote from there would not be released until the invasion had safely begun. Then there would be silence, but from time to time I should receive a 'chit' from regimental HQ to say that all was well.

Neither of us slept much. It seemed ominous that the hotel was in Glasgow's George Square, and we had met six and a half years previously in George Square in Edinburgh. I still have the receipted hotel bill for that night. Leslie thrust it into my hand, thinking that I might want to keep it – surely a prophetic gesture. I was determined that I would not weep or make the parting harder for him, and I managed to say goodbye taut and dry-eyed. I seemed to be standing outside myself and observing, as often one does on the most dramatic occasions of life. Leslie did not want me to go with him to the station, and so I watched him from the hotel-room window, his jaunty walk bravely exaggerated. He did not look back.

Now that I could weep, I did not; that would come later. Rather, I felt a strange exaltation that our brief married life together – consisting of but a few short leaves – had been of such ravishing sweetness, and that I had not spoiled it as I had spoiled things over two years before. I had one letter, written after he got back to Darvel, in which he spoke of how our parting had affected him: 'You seemed so big-eyed and pathetic when I left, that it fairly caught my heart; that exit was the most difficult I've ever made in my life.' Then, after D-Day, came a batch from the sealed camp which, I learned later, was at Fairford airfield near Cirencester in Gloucestershire, and was nicknamed 'The Cage'.

Letters from the sealed camp bore the RAF censor's stamp: clearly, after briefing, even the officers of the SAS were not allowed to censor their own and their men's letters. When briefed, they were behind barbed wire and really were caged in. Tension would then have been growing by the hour, and it must have been hard indeed for the men to keep themselves from being over-stressed by apprehension and excitement. Sport was the obvious cooler. Under canvas, and on the verge of their great adventure, they lived a *Boy's Own Paper* existence. Leslie wrote: 'Last night we had a game of cricket – officers versus sergeants. It was very primitive, but lots of fun. I was dotting about behind the wicket. It is tropically hot, and my sunburn is coming back. I've only to close my eyes and relax a bit to imagine myself back in Africa – except that the indefinable Eastern smell is missing.' This fine weather was not to last – with tragic consequences.

Then there surfaced that seriousness which always lay beneath Leslie's cheerfulness and exuberance:

> My one ambition is to make you as completely happy as I can. And, darling, if I make you half as happy as you make me I shall have done well . . . Bless you, my own darling wife, for being what you are to me – just everything. I believe there's a new film called 'Tender Comrade' – that title begins to express it; it's the comrade in you that makes our passion so deep and yet so clear . . . Dear love, I get plenty of time to think about *us* these days, and I'm more than ever grateful that I have been given such a wonderful person as you to be my wife. I love you utterly and completely, and you give real meaning to life. Darling, you're in my blood, and there aren't any words to express properly all the wonder of you. And not the least wonderful thing is that you let me follow my star,

and encourage me and help me; so many women wouldn't. I hope you feel that I always let you follow yours, because, darling, your opinion on things affecting you and me, or either of us, I think important above all . . . you're a bright star to march upon, and I'm setting a steady pace.

The last letter, bearing the date 8 June, read: 'My heart is very full this evening – a letter from you has just come in, and that brings you even closer to me. I love you so much that I just can't express it in words. My eyes and hands may do that for me, so think of them as you know them . . . I enclose an Order of the Day. Paragraph four fairly hit me in the eye!' Paragraph four of General Montgomery's personal message to the men of 21st Army Group was a verse from Montrose's 'My Dear and Only Love':

> He either fears his Fate too much,
> Or his Deserts are small,
> That puts it not unto the Touch,
> To win or lose it all.

To win or lose it all? Who Dares Wins, I thought: it was the motto of the SAS. 'I take it,' wrote Leslie, 'as a good omen.'

CHAPTER 14

Therefore the Love which doth us bind,
But Fate so obviously debarrs,
Is the Conjunction of the Mind,
And Opposition of the Stars.
      ANDREW MARVELL: 'DEFINITION OF LOVE'

The dread excitement of D-Day came, and I longed to be at Bletchley where I felt I had had a role. I was very lonely in Edinburgh, as none of my friends there was personally involved in the invasion. For about a fortnight there was no news. Then from the sealed camp at Fairford – 'The Cage', where members of the SAS were confined after they had been briefed – there was released the batch of letters to overwhelm me anew with love and foreboding. Another three weeks passed as I waited for the reassuring 'chit'. Since we had no home of our own, any official communication would go to Leslie's mother's address.

On 15 July 1944 the telephone rang and my mother-in-law's voice, hoarse and rasping, gasped out: 'Leslie's missing!' The world spun round, righted itself, and was still; drained of all colour, a spectral landscape. Missing. MISSING. Not dead. Oh, please God, not DEAD. Yet I think I knew, at that moment, that he was dead. That fatal happiness! But hope, desperate and defiant, sprang up at once. He might be a prisoner of war. Yes, surely he was a prisoner of war! I read the telegram in disbelief:

NOTIFICATION RECEIVED FROM NORTH-WEST EUROPE THAT LIEUT L. G. CAIRNS ARMY AIR CORPS WAS REPORTED MISSING ON 17TH JUNE 1944. THE

ENIGMA VARIATIONS

ARMY COUNCIL EXPRESSES SYMPATHY. LETTER
FOLLOWS SHORTLY.

UNDER SECRETARY FOR WAR

The following morning I went with my mother to the foot of the
Pentland Hills near Allermuir, where Leslie and I used so often to
walk, and there we paced up and down, talking and talking. Then I
went back to work.

A few days later I received a letter from Leslie's commanding
officer. It was dated 10 July:

> I imagine by now you have received official notification that
> Leslie is missing. We are all terribly sorry and worried about
> this, as we don't know what has happened. On the 17th day
> of June he left by plane with his section to join his squadron
> commander in France. The plane did not return and we have
> not been able to find out what happened. The plane might
> have been forced down by fighters or other enemy action, or
> had to land for some other reason, and we don't know
> whether the men were able to get away all right or not.
>
> Leslie had a very good lot of men in his section, some of
> them had been with us for a long time. If they got out of the
> plane, they will probably be hiding now and trying to make
> their way back.
>
> I am terribly sorry this should have happened and I
> sincerely hope that we hear from them. I needn't tell you how
> well we all like your husband.
>
> Yours sincerely,
> R.B. Mayne

The administrative officer of 'A' Squadron, Lieut John Todd, in a letter
written towards the end of July, told me that Leslie's aircraft was one
of several which had dropped men in France on 17 June, and that the
other planes had accomplished their mission successfully and had
returned safely to base. When the chaplain, Fraser McLuskey, came
home on leave from France he visited Leslie's mother and me. In
answer to our persistent questioning, he bravely confessed the truth

we had asked for – that Leslie and his men, in spite of the fact that they were wearing uniform, might have been shot as *franc-tireurs*. This possibility was confirmed some months later when I received a letter from the mother of one of the men in Leslie's 'stick' (as a unit of paratroops dropped together from one aircraft was called). Referring to a comrade of her son's, she wrote: 'This boy and mine were together all through the African war and only separated when they were preparing for France. He was a good boy, so happy and carefree, and what an end! He, along with others, was captured in France, held for eight days, and then shot. His poor mother is heart-broken.' So in the summer of 1944, as a result of information supplied by the regiment, I had the impression that Leslie and his men had actually dropped into France, and that their fate thereafter was unknown.

In August 1941 Dr Waltzog of the Legal Department of the German High Command, stated that: 'At the beginning of this war the opinion was held abroad that the German parachutists were not legal combatants but *franc-tireurs* or spies. This is incorrect. Parachute units are part of the German Armed Forces and belong to the Luftwaffe. Members of these units are legal combatants and undertake legitimate military tasks. Their combatant status is the same whether they are employed at the front or behind it . . . As soldiers they wear the uniform given to them and which was made known to the enemy.' Yet Hitler himself referred to the SAS as 'so-called commandos who are recruited in part from common criminals released from prison . . . captured SAS troops must be handed over at once to the nearest Gestapo unit . . . these men are very dangerous, and the presence of SAS troops must be immediately reported . . . they must be ruthlessly exterminated.' That this order was sometimes carried out is now confirmed in *The Secret Hunters* by Anthony Kemp (1986), where it is revealed that on Operation Loyton, to quote one example, captured SAS soldiers were shot in the locality of Moussey, between Luneville and Strasbourg. Moreover, the entire male population of Moussey (210 persons) was taken to a concentration camp as a reprisal for sheltering SAS men; only 70 came back.

Of the SAS, operating in enemy-occupied territory in small groups, unable to be entirely confident of their Maquis contacts and with the Gestapo as a constant threat, a special kind of courage was demanded.

Though there was undoubtedly comradeship, there was also the danger of loneliness and individual enterprise. Their service was of a different order from that of soldiers fighting in bigger, regular units, who shared, by and large, the same collective experiences. In September 1944 Lieutenant-General (Sir) Frederick 'Boy' Browning broadcast to SAS troops behind the German lines. 'It is considered,' he said, 'that the operations you have carried out have had more effect in hastening the disintegration of the German Seventh and Fifth Armies than any other single effort in the army. Considering the numbers involved, you have done a job of work which has had a most telling effect on the enemy and which, I fully believe, no other troops in the world could have done. I know the strain has been great because operating as you do entails the most constant vigilance and cunning which no other troops are called upon to display.'

★★★

I do not know how I came through the next few months – but, yes, I do. Like most people who have had a supremely happy relationship, I felt an aura of love still about me, and Leslie's courage put upon me an obligation to be brave. So did his mother's magnificent fortitude. There was at the time a French popular song, wistful and haunting, and I used to repeat it in my mind like a rosary:

> *J'attendrai –*
> *Le jour et la nuit,*
> *J'attendrai toujours*
> *Ton retour . . .*

I was greatly helped by both our families and by a university friend, Flora Christina (Ena) Macraild, a rumbustious and stout-hearted Celt from Dunvegan in Skye, who listened with endless patience and compassion while I went over and over and over both hopeful and dire possibilities. I was supported in almost equal measure by a new-found friend. When I came back from Bletchley, I had agreed to tutor for the First Ordinary English class at Edinburgh University a Polish woman considerably older than myself. Rozalia Niedzwiedz and I took to each other at once. The daughter of a rich Jewish textile manufacturer from Lodz, this highly intelligent woman of great charm and style had been living in Germany during the years when Hitler was coming to power, and the persecution of Jews had begun. Along with her husband, she escaped to Britain in 1938 but, sadly, her marriage failed. Now penurious ('I live,' she said, 'from mouth to hand'), and accepting her situation with great dignity and courage, she was striving to fulfil her ambition of taking the degree denied to her on the grounds of race years earlier at the University of Cracow.

Once or twice during one of my tutorials with my Polish pupil, Leslie telephoned from Darvel to say that he would shortly be in Edinburgh. Roza – I had learned to call her by this affectionate diminutive – at once sprang to her feet: 'Husband come. I go!' And nothing would detain her. She and Leslie never met. At the time when he was posted missing, she was in a fever of anxiety about her own family who were in the concentration camp at Treblinka, and even then being sent to the gas chambers. She did not refer to her anguish; nor did she to mine, but she bent all her energies towards distracting me, insofar as that was possible. She urged me to go with her to concerts and the theatre, and took me as her guest to the Edinburgh International Club which, owing to the presence of so many servicemen from overseas, was then an active and flourishing society. Sensitively and unobtrusively, she gave me love and support, and perhaps, in turn, I helped a little to divert the course of her suffering. We remained devoted friends for the rest of her life.

In stark contrast to such kindness and understanding was my purgatory at work. My immediate superior in the Department of Agriculture for Scotland, George S—, was openly hostile to the two women graduates in his section, but especially so to me. In the circumstances, his behaviour seemed incomprehensibly cruel. He nit-picked and found unnecessary fault with everything I did. This I endured for several months, having no spirit even to complain. On one occasion, when a breeze from an open window ruffled his papers, Mr S— made a menacing lunge across the desk and shouted, his eyes blazing, 'Did YOU . . .!' and then he stopped, as if even he had seen the absurdity of his conduct. Such manic behaviour I should have found disturbing in normal circumstances, but in my state of extreme tension it had become quite insupportable.

At last I felt I must take action, and I went to the Establishment Branch to ask for a transfer. Even then I stopped short of making a complaint. Hugh Ritchie, the Departmental Officer one rank above Mr S—, a kind and gentlemanly character with whom I always had rapport, sent for me and asked why I wanted to leave. He would not let me off the hook until I had confessed that I could no longer work with my boss. Ritchie admitted that the offending officer got on his nerves too, and begged me to reconsider and to allow him to intervene. I was persuaded against my better judgement to withdraw my request for a transfer. Mr S— was reprimanded and thereafter became quite sycophantic, which made matters almost equally uncomfortable. This behaviour, lasting as it did throughout the months when I was most tortured, was itself a minor enigma. I could not understand how anyone could act as this man did towards another human being suffering as I then was. Perhaps the explanation lay in the fact that he was a person of limited ability, promoted rather too far on account of the war. I could conclude only that he was finding the job too big for him, and was himself under stress, which he relieved by persecuting a subordinate who was particularly vulnerable.

★ ★ ★

As Leslie was the only officer in the missing plane (ironically the transport aircraft was a Stirling – the same name as his birthplace), I decided that I must take the lead among the families. I felt that this was what Leslie would have wanted me to do, for he always cared greatly about the welfare of his men. I obtained the names and addresses of all the next-of-kin. The men in his 'stick' had homes in all parts of the United Kingdom. There were two sergeants: a Welshman from Bridgend, Glamorgan, and an Englishman from Leicester. Both corporals were Scots, from Aberdeen and Edinburgh, and a lance-corporal belonged to Manchester. The troopers came from Yorkshire, the Midlands, the Home Counties, Hampshire, Ulster and even from Co. Waterford in the Republic of Ireland. There were also two men from nearer home: from Polmont near Falkirk, and from

Helensburgh. I contacted their next-of-kin and I undertook to pass on any scraps of information, or even rumour, that I could glean from every possible source. Leslie's mother and I visited the family of the corporal from Edinburgh; and when the mother of a Manchester man came to Edinburgh to stay with friends some time later, we went to see her, too. The writing over the next few months of very many letters to these poor people who were as anguished as I was myself, afforded some distraction and mitigated my feelings of isolation. I bombarded the War Office and importuned the Red Cross; but all to no avail. Later I even appealed to the Member of Parliament for South Edinburgh, then the redoubtable Sir Will Y. Darling, who always made much of his role as an old soldier, to use his position to find out what he could; but he could find nothing.

I was afraid to leave Edinburgh, even momentarily, in case there was word from the War Office, but in September 1944 my mother persuaded me to go with her to Bedford for a short holiday. She thought I should be able to have the company of some of my Bletchley friends. We chose Bedford as it was almost the only place in the locality where hotel accommodation was available. The venture was not a success. Every moment I was in a fever of anxiety lest I should be missing, by so much as a second, the vital news I both longed for and dreaded. I could not go inside BP, as I no longer had a security pass. Wendy was still living in Old Wolverton, and because of her shift work I did not see her very often; and most of those with whom I had been friendliest were billeted in outlying areas. I felt very much on the outside. Worst of all, while I was in Bedford there came news of the disaster at Arnhem, with its tragic loss of parachute and glider-borne troops, of whom so many were posted as missing, and my imagination was set working yet more frenziedly. Of course we now know that the intelligence Ultra was providing should have made the Allied High Command – too complacent and over-confident – much more wary of committing their lightly armed airborne forces to Operation Market Garden. Bletchley's supply of intelligence on the eve of Arnhem was misinterpreted and even ignored.

About two months after I had returned home, a letter came from Angela Woodin at Bletchley; she was someone I had wanted to see but had not had the opportunity:

I have waited a long time before writing to you, hoping all the time that I might hear good news of Leslie from Wendy. You poor little dear —my heart goes out to you, waiting all this time. I know only too well how desperately anxious you must be. I wish I could help you and give you a little comfort. It is all so hard to understand. One can only just go on hoping and praying that it is the best and not the worst that has happened. It seems all so mysterious – I cannot understand why you have heard nothing . . . All I can say to you is that if it is to be good news, it would give me more pleasure than I can say; and if it is bad – I have gone through it, and Anne, and many others, and one does survive and go on, though you think you never will . . . I send you my love and thoughts, and God grant the news may be good when it comes.

★ ★ ★

News did not come, but VE-Day did, and I have to confess that it was one of the saddest days of my life. I wished again that I had been at BP with Angela and Anne and Wendy and my other 'comrades'. But, even there I knew that I could not have rejoiced. While the war continued I could (almost) fool myself into believing that I was like those other women who were merely separated from their men 'for the duration' – or, if not that, at least I felt that my life was suspended. But with the coming of peace, I realised that I should have to face a new, strange, 'normal' world – alone. I stayed close at home that Victory Day as the bells rang out, unable to bear the noisy hilarity of the streets. It was indeed for me, in the words of St John of the Cross, the dark night of the soul.

However, the ending of the war in Europe revived a wraith of hope. Perhaps news could now come through. I inserted the following advertisement in the personal column of *The Times*:

> SAS repatriated prisoners having any INFORMATION about Lieutenant LESLIE GEORGE CAIRNS, 1st SAS Regiment, reported missing over France with 21 other men on June 17, 1944, are earnestly entreated to communicate with Mrs Cairns, 21 Thirlestane Road, Edinburgh.

There was no response and the only result was a paragraph in the *Edinburgh Evening News*:

AIR CRASH MYSTERY
22 Missing for a Year

An aeroplane taking 22 men of the Special Air Service Regiment in June 1944 to be dropped behind the German lines to join the Maquis was recalled on account of bad weather, crashed somewhere in the wooded area near Dijon and no trace has since been found of the plane and its company. This is revealed today by the appeal of Mrs Cairns, of 21 Thirlestane Road, Edinburgh, wife of Lieutenant L.G. Cairns, to repatriated prisoners of war who may have information.

The *Evening News* reporter seemed to have more exact information than either myself or the War Office. Up till then, there had been no official suggestion of the plane's being recalled, and I had been inclined to believe that Leslie had landed in France and had subsequently disappeared.

At about this time the wife of one of Leslie's men, anticipating the ultimate verdict, sent me a highly elaborate printed card intended as an acknowledgement of condolence on the loss of her husband. In its varied typefaces, its symbols of mourning – lilies, the reaping sickle, the portrait photograph framed in lines as if hanging on a wall – and its verses from Longfellow, this seemed an almost Victorian celebration of death. This touching but morbid In Memoriam served only to bring home to me the realisation of what now seemed inevitable.

★ ★ ★

In July 1945 I met Joe Gardner, Leslie's surviving South African cousin. Joe, of the Transvaal Scottish, had been captured at Sidi Resegh in the same action in which his brother Ernest had been killed. He was now being repatriated from Germany via Britain, and had come to Edinburgh to visit his aunt, my mother-in-law. Joe was the antithesis of Leslie – big and blond, with considerable colonial *machismo*. At this time, however, his confidence was very much deflated by an anonymous letter he had received in prison camp concerning his wife. He poured out his heart to me. Instead of rejoicing at his release and the prospect of going home, in his unbalanced mental state he spoke of staying in Britain – with me! I quickly talked him out of that, telling him that he must find out the truth before passing judgment, and reminding him that he had had a good marriage. Later, from South Africa, he wrote to thank me for this advice, but now he reciprocated by telling me, with great gentleness, that I should not go on hoping, as he himself had searched the POW lists and Leslie's name was not on any of them.

Three months later, in October 1945, 16 months from the night when Leslie's plane took off, came the cold official presumption of death:

> Madam,
>
> With reference to War Office letter of 3rd March 1945 regarding your husband Lieutenant L.G. Cairns, Army Air Corps, I am directed to inform you that in view of the length of time which has elapsed since Lieutenant Cairns was reported missing, during which no news of him has been received from any source, the Department has reluctantly, and with deep regret, reached the conclusion that he lost his life. It is consequently being officially recorded that Lieutenant L.G. Cairns, Army Air Corps, is presumed to have been killed in action on the 17th of June 1944.
>
> I am to convey to you an expression of the sincere sympathy of the Army Council.
>
> > I am, Madam,
> > Your obedient servant . . .

This last enigma – the enigma of his fate – would remain. But I had now finally to conclude that the love and the joy and the laughter that was Leslie had vanished for ever.

CHAPTER 15

Brightness falls from the air;
        THOMAS NASHE: 'IN TIME OF PESTILENCE'

Heureux qui comme Ulysse a fait un beau voyage . . .
        JOACHIM DU BELLAY: SONNET

Despite being one of the earliest volunteers of the war, Leslie died a junior officer. Idealism, and the quest for action, drove him to change regiments and branches of the service, and so lose chances of promotion beyond the rank of subaltern. But about this he did not care. Years previously, as a probationary cadet at Harrogate, and later at OCTU, he had said that he would like to make a success of soldiering, but not for the sake of prestige or promotion. This was part of the enigma in his character. In 1940 he had been quite prepared, if need be, to serve in a dangerous capacity in the ranks because he felt he could be more useful in such a role at that critical moment in the country's affairs, rather than go through the extra time and training there and then for a commission. Active and vital service seemed more important than the first pip. Indeed, he did not fight

> For pay and medals, name and rank,
> Things that he has not found . . .

I could not weep, though grief lay on my heart like a heavy stone. I had withheld my tears for too long. Rather I found relief in desperately scribbling poetry, the style and substance a strange mixture of John Pudney, one of the war's best-known poets, and the residual Platonism of one of my university courses. Such was this verse of mine dating from that time:

> My soul you caught
> In your soul's chariot;
> My timid, yearning soul
> Was with a splendid radiance made whole.
>
> Your smoke-brown eyes,
> Joyously wise,
> Your brilliant innocence
> Made synthesis of all experience.
>
> Breath spent, and last words spoken,
> The pattern broken,
> Its archetype I find
> Luminous in the darkness of my mind.

I derived great comfort, too, from the 'real' poetry I loved and knew by heart, and which now encapsulated my desolation. As I crossed North Bridge each day on my way to the dreariness of St Andrew's House, I used to look across the cold Firth of Forth, and Housman's lines hammered in my brain:

> As past the plunge of plummet,
> In seas I cannot sound,
> My heart and soul, and senses,
> World without end, are drowned.
>
> Here by the labouring highway
> With empty hands I stroll:
> Sea-deep, till doomsday morning,
> Lie lost my heart and soul.

Leslie had left no letter for me to read in the event of his death. What more would there have been to say? He had expressed so often the depth of his love and had made it clear to me that I had given meaning to his life. He would not have presumed to tell me how to conduct the remainder of mine. One of my friends said he was a romantic boy who thought he bore a charmed life, but I argued that this was a superficial judgment. Romantic he certainly was, but I feel there was a deeper layer of consciousness from which he had decided to take a calculated risk, fully believing he would survive. No one was more eager for life, and none better equipped to live it fully. Long ago, when he was a cadet at OCTU, he had written: 'I feel such an ache of longing for you. After it's all over, we'll never allow ourselves to be separated again . . . I shan't mind this war a bit, if it allows us – and especially you – to live a free and peaceful life afterwards.'

Somehow I had to be worthy of this sacrifice; to make my life count, if only a little. I would leave this drab and unhappy employment in St Andrew's House – for what I did not yet know. All I had was a testimonial from Harold Fletcher of GCHQ, which was no testimonial in that it gave a potential employer absolutely no enlightenment because it could not do so:

> Mrs Cairns was engaged on work of a secret nature; the
> Official Secrets Acts preclude the giving of any information
> in connection with her duties.

But first I would make one further effort to solve the last enigma: to find out what had happened to Leslie. I would go to France, and there make enquiries at the Ministière de la Défence Nationale in Paris.

★ ★ ★

Travel abroad for middle-class young people before student age was relatively uncommon up until the war, and during hostilities only service personnel and those on official government business were permitted to leave these shores. Had circumstances been different, I should probably have travelled in Europe during my university days. Even within Great Britain, pre-war holidays for Scottish families were usually taken in the Highlands or at nearby seaside resorts. This state of things must indeed seem strange to the young people of today who can fly off for a summer in Katmandu with scarcely a quiver of apprehension or pause for wonder. At Bletchley I had begun to satisfy, however pathetically or inadequately, a desire to see the world about me, but then had neither the time nor the money nor the opportunity for anything other than very restricted local journeys. Besides, the propaganda slogan 'Is Your Journey Really Necessary?' was fretted into one's mind.

Now it was possible to travel to certain parts of Europe. Paris would definitely be an adventure, especially since I would be going alone. Roza Niedzwiedz would gladly have come with me but, as an alien, she feared she would not be granted re-entry into Britain. She was, however, immensely enthusiastic and encouraging, trying to make me think of the enterprise as a holiday as well as a mission with a sad and serious purpose. From her knowledge of the continent she was able to give me useful information, advice and travellers' tips, and she suggested that I take with me a supply of those items which were in even shorter supply in France than in Britain, such as coffee and cigarettes, and use them as barter. I followed this recommendation but, not having a very developed commercial instinct, I was glad to make gifts to the various people who were kind to me.

I applied for leave and departed from Victoria Station on 15 September 1946, on the famous Golden Arrow train, which on the other side of the Channel became the *Flèche d'Or*. As the white cliffs of Dover receded and the coast of France drew near, the inimitable excitement of 'abroad' took hold of me for the first time – the only positive emotion I had felt for 26 months.

At Calais the peg-legged porter unloading the baggage with as much agility as his able-bodied fellows became, in my overheated imagination, a victim of Verdun, and such was the exotic evocation of 'foreign soil', that I think I expected northern France to be totally distinct from southern England – almost like another planet. But, apart from the devastation, especially in the harbour area, the only real dissimilarities I noticed were the shutters on the houses and the fact that the dwellings were all taller and narrower than in England. I assumed that this was more than an architectural whim, but might have some connection with conservation of land in this predominantly agricultural country.

I was not due to arrive in Paris until very late in the evening, when it would be dark. Some girls I knew had arranged for their two pen-friends to meet me at the Gare du Nord and, somehow, we recognised one another. I am sure that, looking lost, I was not difficult to identify. The girls bore me off immediately for a welcoming glass of wine. Tiredness, the excitement of the journey and of sitting, so late, at a pavement café such as I had seen only in films (these agreeable continental institutions had not yet spread to London, far less pre-Festival Edinburgh), as well as the unaccustomed intake of alcohol, all made my head reel. I was very glad that my acquaintances escorted me to the Metro, with instructions to change at Dentfert-Rochereau for the Cité Universitaire, where I had managed to book a room in the Pavillon Franco-Britannique. I have no recollection of how I found my way there in the dark, but I do remember having to knock up the concièrge, who grumbled in just the style portrayed in the cinema. My room was bare indeed, with merely a bed, no pillow, and one rough blanket; the Germans had pillaged everything else. Nonetheless, I fell almost at once into an exhausted sleep.

The next morning I went for breakfast to the vast central cafeteria which served all the national pavilions. It was crammed with students, some on vacation courses; the number of students in Paris has always been enormous. As I entered the building a chant started up, but I could not catch the words. The vociferation grew louder and louder all the time while I was serving myself at the counter. As I sat down, my neighbour whispered to me, '*Otez votre chapeau!*' Mystified, I took off the small velvet beret I was wearing and, miraculously, the vast hall was quiet, and I learned that the chant had been '*Cha*-peau! *Cha*-peau!' Apparently, to wear a hat in the cafeteria was a student shibboleth. H.M. Bateman's little man did not have that particular situation to face.

After breakfast I ventured forth and was at once overwhelmed by the beauty and the scale of the buildings. London was, of course, by far the larger city, but much of London's majesty had been destroyed in the Blitz. Paris gave the immediate illusion of spaciousness and grandeur; the swelling pride of Louis XIV and Napoleon had expressed itself in truly monumental architecture. Now, having seen other great cities of the world, I am inclined to have warmer feelings towards those of more human proportion, or those which are, like

Rome, a palimpsest. I noted the small bunches of flowers laid in the Place de la Concorde in memory of Resistance fighters, and thought, how especially fragile and touching they seemed in the immensity of that noble square. The august length of the Champs Elysées culminating in the sublime Arc de Triomphe with the eternal flame burning beneath it could not but fill me with reverential awe. Awe of a different order touched me as I observed the intimidatingly sybaritic cafés lining the avenue, and I was almost overcome with a *crise de nerfs* when attempting to cross at Etoile. But the river – the river was something else! The mighty Thames had dignity and sober beauty but, despite Wordsworth's sonnet, I always thought of it as business-like, the powerful engine-room of the city. The Seine, on the contrary, was fantasy. Those islands! Always I had found magic in small islands, and here was one with a full-rigged galleon of a cathedral as if moored alongside.

The Rive Gauche fascinated me, with its bookstalls ready to yield a treasure trove to the discerning, sharp-eyed bibliophile; and I was amused by the artists, painting in attitudes varying from complete absorption to self-conscious posturing bravura. At Montmartre, I was disappointed by the Sacré Coeur, and I dared, privately, to categorise it as vulgar; but, of course, I was quite unused to Second Empire Romanesque, and knew only the filigree stonework of English Gothic, and now the glorious tracery and the flying buttresses of Nôtre Dame. But the ambience called up the shades of Toulouse-Lautrec and Gaugin, and of Mimi, and these began to work their fermentation in my imagination.

★ ★ ★

I had an introduction to the Revd Dr Donald Caskie, minister of the Scots Kirk in the rue Bayard. At the fall of France, Donald Caskie had refused a place on the last boat home and instead had gone south where, working from the Seamen's Mission in Marseilles, he had hidden hundreds of allied servicemen and helped them to escape over the Pyrenees into Spain. He was arrested and tortured in German and Italian prisons, and once was confined in a bottle-dungeon in which he could neither sit nor stand up. Yet his Christian faith never wavered.

He was condemned to death, and saved only by the intervention of a German padre. Now back in the manse at 4 rue Piccini, on certain evenings he kept open house for young people of all nationalities. Edinburgh friends who knew him from his Islay childhood thought that he might be able to help me.

I went to the manse, a beautiful flat near the avenue Foche, and the door was opened by a grave and courteous manservant. When I had told my story to the minister, he introduced me to Ivan Feigelson (known to his friends as Ika), a young medical student of Russian emigré parentage. Along with General de Gaulle's nephew Pierre, Ika had organised from Grenoble, in co-operation with the Maquis, the transmission of intelligence to the general himself, who at that time was in command of the Free French forces in the area. Both boys had been taken prisoner and tortured (according to Dr Caskie, who told the story in his book *The Tartan Pimpernel*) 'until the blood came out of their ears'; but they managed convincingly to deny their activities, and eventually they were released.

I found Ika a kind and gentle young man. He said: 'Your husband would have been one of us. Would you like me to go with you to make enquiries at the War Office?' Of course I said that I would, and Ika arranged an appointment for me. A minor official – quite remarkably almost a caricature Frenchman – condescended to see us. Too obviously he had lunched well on a dish laced with garlic, and he kept twirling his dark moustache, of which he seemed inordinately proud, while in halting French I explained my purpose. The official appeared to ponder —I had the feeling that the pause was histrionic rather than meditative – and I was aware that he had no real concern. When at last he spoke, the words were spat out in sharp interrogation. I was glad of Ika's presence to support me and supplement my responses:

'Where was your husband to be dropped?'

'Whom among the Maquis was he to contact?'

'What was your husband's code-name?'

From this last question I realised that he thought Leslie had been a member of the Special Operations Executive (SOE), whose agents, trained in Britain and flown or dropped into France, worked in association with local groups and sent back information to London. ('A' Squadron of the SAS had indeed had some contact with SOE agents in the Morvan, but the principal nature of their work had been somewhat different.) When I explained that my husband had been a member of the British armed forces and was in uniform, the official seemed to lose all interest, which I thought strange, as there had been French and Belgian equivalents of the SAS in 1944. When it became clear that he had nothing to tell me, I made my exit in the face of dismissive politeness. So ended – for the moment – my quest to solve the last enigma.

Ika, however, did not dismiss me. He invited me several times to supper at his parents' house. I was very grateful –for the company, chiefly, though I found conversation difficult with M and Mme Fiegelson, who spoke French with a heavy Russian accent. Ika, however, had a brilliant command of English, to which he was to add proficiency in several other languages during the years when he practised as a noted paediatrician in Paris. Though never a gourmet, I appreciated also the food at Ika's home, as I found what was provided at the Cité Universitaire almost inedible, even accustomed as we in Britain were to such unappetising fare as powdered egg and cakes baked with liquid paraffin. The soup was a nauseous fluid resembling dirty dishwater, and it upset my stomach; and the ersatz coffee, made from ground acorns, was very evil-tasting. Fiercely anti-Vichy, Ika's family had considered it patriotic to have duplicate ration books; these they had conveniently retained in a post-Vichy world and so they wanted for little.

An artist I met that evening at Dr Caskie's suggested that I exchange my tourist food permit for a civil emergency ration card, and do my own marketing and cooking. She kindly lent me dishes and pans, which were almost unobtainable, and in any case needed coupons for their purchase. I took her advice but, still not a skilled cook, and reluctant to waste time queuing for the use of the small gas-ring in the basement of the pavilion at the Cité Universitaire, I lived on bread and fruit, and on eggs, which could sometimes be bought, hard-boiled, from stalls in the streets. Luckily, I did not become jaundiced by this diet.

Corruption was rife in France; bribery and the black market were more widespread and unconcealed than in Britain. Clothing was rationed, as it was at home, but without a 'textile ticket' one could quite easily obtain goods in the regular shops by openly paying the assistant a bribe. I was offered a pair of shoes for about one third more than the market price, and I was so much in need of shoes that I fell into temptation. I got my deserts, however, when being shown the sights of Paris by a distinguished professor and holder of the Légion d'Honneur, to whom my cousin had given me an introduction. I was wearing the shoes, as ill-fitting as ill-gotten, and the pain in my feet as I pounded the pavements was excruciating. I was too embarrassed to confess my sin and suffered in guilty silence.

Roza had insisted that I sample some of the frivolities of Paris. I did not really have the heart for such things, but I knew I should be interrogated on my return, and I was aware that she was merely trying hard to push me into normal post-war life. And so I decided to patronise the famous Café de la Paix; but having little money and no head for alcohol, limited myself to ordering Perrier before lunch, and sat at a table on the pavement, watching the world go by. There were no tourists, and my air of demure solitariness must have been conspicuous, for I attracted the attention of a man whom I then thought of as middle aged, and who was of distinctly raffish appearance. He came and sat down beside me and offered to show me the sights. I was not quite so lacking in worldly wisdom, however, as to accept his invitation, whereupon he gave me his card – but I did not pursue the acquaintance.

The other compulsory flippant activity was a visit to Antoine, the famous hairdresser who, Roza told me, had a salon at number 5 rue Cambon. (Roza, in her more affluent days, had been accustomed to quite a lot of sophisticated luxury.) I made my way to this celebrated establishment, and was very surprised to find an open salon; we in Britain were at that time still cowering modestly in cubicles. Here I was given one piece of advice: 'For you, the simplest is the best.' A dubious compliment, perhaps, but a precept I have held to ever since.

I took the train to Fontainebleau, and to Versailles, and saw there the famous Hall of Mirrors where the notorious Treaty was signed which set Germany on the path to Hitler's domination and the Second World War. When Ika came to London the following year, he was to describe Buckingham Palace, by comparison, as 'a modest little house'. Then I went to Chartres, where I found the unequal spires of the cathedral strangely homely and appealing after the stately symmetry of Nôtre Dame. Within, the jewelled glass of the great rose window lifted my spirits, and I felt my sorrow melt in the flames of the myriad candles. The gold-shafted darkness seemed redolent of immemorial grief and prayer. Later, back home again, I wrote this verse to express the experience:

> I came to the cathedral,
> Faith-hungry agnostic
> I came with my pain
> Unwept, unacknowledged.
>
> The bright dark revealed it,
> The candle-flames annealed it,
> The windows' jewelled lucence washed it clear;
> And aeons of prayers ascending,
> In anguished spirals blending,
> Distilled it to a tear.

Ika delivered to me an 'express letter' invitation to a party, by means of the Pneumatique — a strange device, comparable, I supposed, to that which sent cash round department stores. I had not been to such a party since before Leslie went to North Africa, and talking to Ika and his friends on a balcony canopied by a starry sky, I felt a spurt of pleasure, quickly followed by a surge of guilt: Leslie was dead, and I alive, and capable of enjoying some temporary diversion. The haunting words of Dowson's poem, which had brought us together again in 1943, returned to me as I stood on that Paris balcony:

> I cried for madder music and for stronger wine,
> But when the feast is finished and the lamps expire,
> Then falls thy shadow, Cynara! the night is thine;
> And I am desolate and sick of an old passion,
>   Yea hungry for the lips of my desire:
> I have been faithful to thee, Cynara! in my fashion.

★ ★ ★

Pangs of conscience and ache of loneliness apart, I found that I was stimulated by the challenge of finding my way about this great and beautiful city, and by having to communicate – to try to speak French quickly enough to make actual conversation possible. At the end of my stay I felt almost at home in the country and the language. Paris began the slow healing process. I realised that life might still hold some pleasure, if not happiness. Like Ulysses, I had, by my standards then, made *un beau voyage*, but I did not think it would result in my being content to stay at home thereafter.

* * *

But Paris had not solved the last enigma. There were still so many terrible possibilities. Had the plane been recalled on account of bad weather and plunged into the sea? Or had it been shot down over the Channel? Did it come down in remote forest land where it still lay, gradually decaying? Had the plane, crippled by flak, crash-landed, and its occupants been killed, or, having survived, been tortured and perhaps shot? Had the men escaped and dispersed, meeting divers fates? Surely, then, word would have been heard of some of them. Even the wild surmise occurred to me that Leslie might have lost his memory; but common sense reasserted itself, and I realised that this could not have been the fate of all his men.

I could not fail to speculate about what might have happened had Leslie remained in his original regiment. The Ayrshire Yeomanry had experienced an active enough war after all. In the battle for Tunis the 152nd had lost two commanding officers in three days; and in Italy they had fought with the Guards in bloody actions from Cassino to the Po. Leslie could have participated in battles on historic ground, and perhaps not have lost his life, but come back to me. Or in North Africa, having left the 11th Field Regiment, he might have sat out the rest of the war in luxury, gaining rank through time and, come the peace, have been a live major instead of a dead lieutenant.

But 'might-have-been' is the most poignant and fruitless of all sentiments, and I could not denigrate Leslie's individualistic choice of combat, nor dismiss as quixotry his response to vision in the conduct of war. I came to believe that in the SAS he had realised his ideal of chivalry in a contemporary setting; and that with our marriage and my acceptance of his decision, the two halves of his nature had come together, and for him that enigma of character had been resolved.

EPILOGUE

Farewell to a name and a number
  Recalled again
To darkness and silence and slumber
  In blood and pain.

So ceases and turns to the thing
  He was born to be
A soldier cheap to the King
  And dear to me;

So smothers in blood the burning
  And flaming flight
Of valour and truth returning
  To dust and night.

A.E. HOUSMAN: *MORE POEMS*, XL

With the Falklands War in 1982 – conventional warfare such as no one expected to see again – there surfaced memories that had never been buried very deep. For many British people of my generation, the sight of great ships sailing for a remote theatre of action, their rails lined with cheering soldiers, at once evoked echoes of convoys leaving for Africa or the Far East, yet at the same time produced surprise at the media coverage and the openness with which these preparatory stages, and indeed the later fighting, appeared to be reported. To one trained in the more-than-circumspect world of Ultra at Bletchley, the press and public expectation of immediate news and information, not just about military successes and casualties, but even about questions of tactics – and that in advance of the action – seemed incomprehensible.

Given that conditions had changed greatly in 40 years, and that 'the right to know' had in every walk of life assumed paramount importance, it seemed nevertheless unrealistic – even allowing for the vastly different scale of the conflict – for relatives of servicemen to protest at lack of information over but a few days or even hours.

Beyond and above the jolt to the national memory, there was for me a special exhumation of the past. The crash of the Sea King helicopter in which 20 members of the SAS died was reported as the regiment's single greatest loss since a whole troop with an aircraft had been posted missing in the Second World War. This referred to Leslie and his men.

Just after the end of the Falklands conflict, my second husband died, suddenly and unexpectedly, almost 40 years to the day after he had been wounded and taken prisoner at Tobruk while serving with the Royal Durban Light Infantry in the ill-fated 2nd South African Division. From the first, he had been selflessly understanding about my own war, and we had had a very happy marriage. We had met in South Africa (where he had been born), had left for political reasons, and had decided to make our home in Edinburgh. He had grown to love the city as I did, and had become, in effect, a Scotsman.

We came to live in the south side of the city and joined the local parish church which, by coincidence, had been Leslie's mother's church; he himself had not been a member, nor had I attended it. My second husband had been born 6,000 miles away, but at his funeral service the coffin lay but a few feet from the church war memorial tablet bearing Leslie's name. It was a Hardyesque situation, and one which added an element of tragic irony to my sorrow. I was devastated. Once again I felt that if I did not somehow sublimate my pain, I should be irretrievably lost.

For some time I had nourished a wish to write a war memoir, and after a while, and with the approach of the fiftieth anniversary of the start of the war, the desire became urgent. I grew to think that to do this would be mind-saving, a catharsis, and, in a strange way, an expurgation of a double grief. This book has been the result. I began to write, not without much heart-searching and some misgiving. I could not bear any imputation of disloyalty to my second husband. I had been devoted to him, and he to me, and he had brought me a happiness I thought never to find again. But, I argued, he had been granted nearly 40 more years of life, and had our son as memorial. Leslie had had nothing. It seemed that I should merely be making the balance even.

★ ★ ★

In my life in wartime there were three enigmas.

When I began to re-read letters, and to research in records, official histories, biographies and first-hand accounts of activities behind the enemy lines in France, it emerged that the last enigma was in fact a double enigma. Not only was Leslie's fate unknown, but there appeared to be considerable confusion in the regimental records and in subsequent references to the operations in which he died. Some things I found led to moments of great distress, as evidence (which I was subsequently able to disprove) suggested the strong possibility of his having been executed by the enemy.

Leslie served in 'A' Squadron of the 1st SAS Regiment. In Operation Houndsworth, 'A' Squadron's allotted task was to establish a base ('Houndsworth') in the mountainous, wooded country south-west of Dijon — the Monts du Morvan in the Département of Nièvre. They were to drop at various locations north of Château-Chinon. Their mission was to cut the railway lines Lyons–Châlon-sur-Saône–Dijon–Paris, and Le Creusot–Nevers, and to keep them out of action by continuing attacks. According to the squadron report, their operations succeeded in blowing up, among others, the Dijon–Beaune line seven times, the Dijon–Paris line twice and the Nevers–Autun track four times. They blew power lines, blocked roads, derailed six trains, destroyed a number of vehicles of various kinds, brought down an enemy aircraft, and killed 220 German troops, including a general. Between two and three thousand Maquis fighters were armed, and captured allied airmen were freed. Valuable information was sent back regarding troop movements, flying-bomb factory and assembly areas, and supply dumps. Targets for RAF bombing raids were pinpointed. Their most spectacular coup by far was the discovery of Rommel's headquarters. All this was achieved at the cost of only two SAS soldiers killed — Captain Roy Bradford and a trooper who was a mechanic for the jeeps, both casualties in the one incident – and seven men wounded. The fate, of course, of Leslie and his men was another matter. However, the area which 'A' Squadron had to cover was far too large, several of their jeeps were lost through parachute failures, and the squadron was greatly hampered from first to last by appalling freak weather conditions.

On checking certain facts in David Buxton's *Honour to the Airborne*, Part II: *Sword of Honour*, I was surprised and distressed to find Leslie's name and those of the men in his 'stick' listed as in 'D' Squadron and as casualties on operation 'Gain'. This work purports to be authoritative, and it is the source relied upon by the SAS Regimental Association when supplying information of the kind which I was now seeking. Apart from the confusion of squadrons, the implications of his having been engaged in this quite different operation were serious. For those given by Buxton as missing on operation 'Gain' – listed by name, rank and number as Leslie and his men – approximates to the total of SAS troops now known to have been captured and executed by the Germans on that operation in the Forêt de Fontainebleau, south of Paris. The conclusion was distressingly obvious. This was the first I had heard of Leslie's alleged connection with 'D' Squadron.

Of course I realised that at the last moment he could have been attached to another troop, but this seemed highly unlikely in view of the SAS methods of training, which relied upon close personal co-operation between all ranks. Fraser McLuskey kindly confirmed my belief that Leslie had indeed been in 'A' Squadron – it was with them that the Padre had dropped into France, and with them that he had carried out his ministry deep behind enemy lines. However, Major John Wiseman, MC, at first told me categorically (in a private communication) that my husband had *not* been in 'A' Squadron, but later kindly wrote to me to correct this statement. A recent correspondence printed in the Regimental Association journal *Mars and Minerva* alluded to the time in Operation Houndsworth when three aircraft had left from Fairford for the Morvan. In his own published letter relating to the episode Major Wiseman stated that three planes had taken off, had been unable to locate the dropping zone, had turned back, and that one had failed to return and 'was presumed shot down in the Channel'. In fact Major Wiseman's letter preserves an inaccurate memory – not surprising after so long – of the actual circumstances, for it conflates the events of 12 days and relates them as if they had happened on the same night. The true facts can be established from examination of the official report on Operation Houndsworth (1st SAS Regimental records, File 214).

The report by 'A' Squadron commander, Major Bill Fraser, MC, contains a diary of the 'Houndsworth' operation. After the arrival in France of the advance reconnaissance party on 6 June 1944, Major Fraser had taken off with the main recce party on 10 June. They had been unable to find the target, but had dropped and had become widely scattered. Over the next few days the local Maquis had gathered them up, somewhat improbably, in a bright red 32-seater bus! A camp was set up in the Bois de Lapiérouse. The diary continues:

> 17th June. Expected 3 planes and arranged reception committee on Les Vellottes.
> 18th June. In the early morning planes were heard passing over in the mist and the rain. They had not seen the flares and turned back . . . Lt. Cairn's [sic] plane failed to return.
> 19th June. The weather appalling. DZ manned again by Lt. Stewart.
> 20th June. DZ at Vieux Dun manned again. Nothing came.
> 22nd June. Captain Bradford, the Padre, Lt. Ball and men dropped successfully at Les Vellottes. Captain Muirhead, Captain Wiseman, Lt. Grayson and the Doctor with men landed at Vieux Dun . . .

That single sentence is the sole mention in the report of the loss of Leslie's aircraft. I knew about the bad weather, and I had learned later that, on account of this, the plane had been recalled without accomplishing its mission. But, as I have said, the impression I was given in 1944 by three officers of the SAS was that Leslie and his men had been dropped, and that only the plane itself had not returned. That was all I ever learned directly from the regiment or from the War Office. It may seem a small point when a man is dead, but all other records have always given 17 June as the presumed date of death. It is only now clear to me that in actual fact it must have been a day later.

Annexed to Major Fraser's general report is a separate report by Captain Muirhead, MC, of 2 Troop:

> 17th June. Took off 2330 hrs. Hit by flak over Caen. Dropping
> area obscured by 10/10th cloud, returned 0600 hrs.

The fact that one of Captain Muirhead's three planes did not return was not mentioned.

The loss of five experienced NCOs in particular was serious. As Philip Warner has said in *The Special Air Service*, the official history re-issued in an expanded edition in 1983, the regiment 'has often been criticised for the high proportion of officers and NCOs, as well as first-class men, which it absorbed, and the answer must invariably be that used in this way they caused far more damage to the enemy than they would have done if they had been with other units. The main drawback to this officer/NCO/soldier ratio was that if a party was killed or taken prisoner the enemy scored a success well out of proportion to the numbers involved.'

There is a mysterious entry in the squadron diary under 18 July. 'Two a/c collided over DZ. 16 bodies were buried.' Here was a further cause for retrospective anxiety which, had I not re-examined Fraser McLuskey's *Parachute Padre*, might have haunted me. Certainly the date was out by exactly one month, but the report offered no explanation as to the identity of these bodies, whether they were connected with the 'collision' (itself not explained), or whether at this date they were chanced upon and were in fact those of Leslie and his 'stick'. No indication was given as to how they might have died. As I considered the contents of the squadron report, it seemed to me that the probability was that the bodies were those of aircrew from supply aircraft, for there was some suggestion in the report that a Liberator and a Halifax had been lost over the Morvan when ferrying supplies; but the point is that no proper statement was ever made in regimental records. Had the bodies been those of the missing SAS troops, I reasoned, then they could no longer have been 'missing', and the Padre would certainly have told me about their discovery. One has to resort to Fraser McLuskey's memoir for the explanation that the bodies were indeed RAF and American crewmen, and for a moving account of their dignified burial by the Padre himself almost within sight of the enemy.

Royal Air Force records are fuller and more accurate than those of the SAS. From these I have learned only very recently that the Stirling concerned (LJ 850) belonged to 620 Squadron. The pilot for the flight on 17 June was an Australian Warrant Officer R.W. Crane. There were in all six of an aircrew, plus an army dispatcher. The records list 15 SAS passengers, but Leslie's name is not mentioned. No one source that I have consulted gives the same total of SAS troops as any other: numbers vary from 15 to 17 men (including the officer). RAF records about the special mission and the destination in the Morvan tally with those of the SAS. Apparently reports from the two other aircraft suggested to the airforce authorities that the plane might have hit high ground, since the cloud-base was very low.

Here further evidence adds a new element to the mystery. It was revealed also by the RAF that when Leslie's plane left Fairford at 23.20 hours on 17 June it had a glider in tow. Nowhere else in the records relating to Operation Houndsworth is a glider mentioned. 'A' Squadron was bound for mountainous, wooded country. It is difficult to conceive how a glider would have been deployed. All the jeeps with their heavy machine-guns mounted fore and aft were dropped by parachute. All the troops came in similar fashion. Supplies, too, were later dropped. Certainly some men of the SAS did (as Captain Derrick Harrison tells us) make a few training flights in gliders when waiting at Fairford to be sent to France; and the use of gliders for later operations was considered. This naturally depended on the terrain: there is no evidence that I can find to suggest that gliders were used in the Morvan on operation Houndsworth. What was this glider doing on an operation in which apparently gliders were not involved? What did it contain? What was the fate of its pilots and its passengers if such there were? Surely an aircraft bound on an important secret mission deep into enemy-held eastern France would not be used simply as a tug for a glider bound for a different, nearer destination – somewhere in Normandy, perhaps – when the lives of the highly skilled parachute troops in that 'tug', and the success of the ultimate SAS operation itself, might be put in jeopardy. What would be the point of a single glider being towed to Normandy 11 days after the invasion and the establishment of a bridgehead for the landing of men and supplies? The Stirling bombers used on the SAS missions such as Houndsworth were more than a local goods service ferrying freight to various points in France.

In his book *This is the SAS* Tony Geraghty twice mentions the disappearance of Leslie's aircraft, and the reader will realise from the context in which Geraghty discusses this incident that a loss of this number of men from a small unit was a serious matter. However, he goes on to say that these men were not counted as casualties in Operation Houndsworth. (It should be noted in passing that yet further confusion – and pain to me – was added by Tony Geraghty's once associating the incident of the missing plane with the unfortunate Operation Loyton, in which the SAS troops posted missing are now known to have been tortured and shot by the Gestapo.) When I asked Tony Geraghty what he had meant by 'not being counted' he pointed out that the SAS's own casualty figures did not add up. He went on to say: 'This is not necessarily sinister. As one of the Ultra team you will recall that precise statistics of our own losses was not always possible. I suspect that SAS casualties (like those of other special forces) suffered from the peculiar problem that many of those wearing the regiment's badge were on the strength of another formation.' This last point is certainly not irrelevant, since the commemorative scroll sent to me from the Palace names Leslie as of the Parachute Regiment; and under this unit did he appear for the last time in the Army List. Yet he is included quite correctly on the Bayeux memorial to the missing as belonging to the SAS. By some error, however, his name is omitted altogether from the Edinburgh University war memorial under the arches of the Old Quad, where daily we used to meet.

Major Wiseman has stated that the plane was presumed shot down over the Channel. There is no suggestion that, though all three aircraft had been it by flak over Caen on the outward journey, Leslie's had come down then. If it had reached the Morvan and had then turned round, but did not make it back to base, then a crash on land or sea is self-evident: if on land, only the agency – the weather, engine trouble, or enemy action – is in doubt. The RAF suspected that the aircraft had hit a hillside. As the weather was so bad – over Normandy conditions deteriorated into the worst storms for 40 years – the likelihood of Luftwaffe fighters being up seems remote; but of course the hazard of anti-aircraft fire was omnipresent. All the troops on board were trained and fully equipped parachutists. In the event of enemy action, surely some, or all, might have been able to bale out if the plane had not immediately exploded. I have already discussed the improbability of the entire aircraft, its crew and its troops disappearing totally over land; though, of course, had it come down in enemy-occupied territory, nothing might ever have been known of the matter if all the occupants had perished, and certainly not if any survivors had been disposed of (which, given the purpose of their mission, would have been highly probable). Nevertheless Fraser McLuskey's account of air crashes does suggest that the Maquis or the local French population in general would soon have known of planes which had come down in their territory, and that the Germans, when told of wrecks, did in fact bury the crews in identifiable graves.

It has interested me very much to learn from the Air Historical Branch of the Royal Air Force that after the war, since nothing had been heard of Warrant Officer Crane's Stirling, its crew and SAS passengers, a search was made of the Morvan region. This was carried out with thoroughness, but without success, by the Missing Research and Enquiry Service, and in 1948 the case was closed. As far as the army was concerned, I had been told in October 1945 that effectively the matter was ended with the presumption of death. I heard no more officially from the regiment, though on return visits to the Morvan area representatives of the SAS will have been anxious to find out anything they could. When he published *Parachute Padre*, Fraser McLuskey mentioned the fact that to that day no trace had been found of the missing plane. Both the air force and the army, as well as those who actually served with Leslie, seemed now to presume that the aircraft had come down in the English Channel.

But what has saddened me especially was the repeated rumour which I and some friends heard in the 1950s and early 1960s: that Leslie's plane had been brought down not by the storms nor by enemy action, but by human error on our own side. The story current was that on its return flight the plane had been fired on mistakenly by a naval vessel in the

Channel – the sea was full of our shipping, of course, in the weeks after D-Day, and there was a corresponding absence of German fighters. I have in fairness to say that there is no hard evidence for this; but it seems possible that if such a case of misidentification had occurred, it would not readily be admitted. Many such things happened, no doubt, during the war. Perhaps the strange lack of concern in 'A' Squadron's diary and reports, and the fact that I heard so little from the regiment subsequently, may reflect a suspicion (or knowledge) on their part. Although this fate, however tragic, would certainly be preferable to possible torture and execution, I know that Leslie himself, who volunteered so often to do something 'useful', would have preferred to be killed actually fighting, like Bradford and Fenwick. His preparing himself so keenly for a new and final phase of the war, and then not seeing even the beginning of it, was the final irony.

All Leslie's letters to me from the sealed camp at Fairford bore (as well as the RAF censor's stamp) undated postmarks. All, that is, save the last. This bore the date 19 June. It had been written on 8 June, and he said quite clearly that it would be his last 'until I see you again'. He always wrote very regularly. What had accounted for the nine-day gap between this date and the night of his eventual departure for France? Had he been, or was he about to be, briefed for a mission earlier than that on which he actually set out? For obvious security reasons no one was briefed earlier than was necessary. A full nine days before a mission was far too long. Perhaps he had believed he was to go with the main reconnaissance party, and having written his last letter did not write to me again to cause me what he thought would be further confusion and anxiety. If he had been briefed for a mission in which he did not participate, he would then have been kept incommunicado until he did finally leave. The reconnaissance party flew safely to France, and dropped successfully, as did all the other teams of 'A' Squadron.

There is no armour against fate: as with the second cousin, so with the fourth.

When Leslie's medals came, long after the war, they included the France and Germany Star. It was ironic, as it must be presumed that he had never set foot on French soil. Or had he . . .?

★ ★ ★

But long ago, in 1946, the questing and the questioning had become almost unbearable, and I knew that to keep my sanity I must force myself to an arbitrary conclusion: I would believe the least terrible of terrible possibilities – that the plane had been shot down over the Channel by enemy action. Early in 1943 Leslie had written to me from North Africa: 'I had the unusual experience of seeing a Messerschmitt 110 shot down by AA fire not 100 feet above my head. It crashed nearby, and started burning – I only hope the poor devils were dead before they hit the deck, although we all instinctively gave a yell of applause, and I felt rather conscience-stricken afterwards.' I prayed then that this merciful fate which Leslie wished for the enemy had been granted also to him.

> So smothers in blood and burning
>   And flaming flight
> Of valour and truth returning
>   To dust and night.

★ ★ ★

In the first flush of youthful passion, and in the imminence of war, Leslie had vowed that he would rather have a few years with me than eternal life without me. At the end of the war I could say that I, too, was prepared to forego a nebulous eternity in exchange for the short span we had had together. But, nevertheless, for me eternity was not now, and I had to go on into the future and in this world. Leslie had taught me how to live, and the war how to endure. The immigrant ship to South Africa, and all that followed, was still in the womb of time; but at that moment I resolved that though I would grieve for Leslie for the rest of my life, I would yet go forward, lighting my way by the torch of the incandescent spirit.

POSTSCRIPT 2000

In the ten years since *Enigma Variations* appeared, the public profiles of both the organisation which broke the German Enigma code and that of the SAS have been considerably heightened.

The books written about Bletchley Park have continued, unsurprisingly, and for the most part, to concentrate on the technology. However, in *Codebreakers* (1993), edited by F.H. Hinsley and Alan Stripp, there are some personal reminiscences, and a disclosure that John Cairncross, the 'Fifth Man', worked at Bletchley from 1942 to 1943. In the same volume a contribution by Peter Gray Lucas appears to correct my assumption, which was held by many at BP, that there was foreknowledge of the bombing of Coventry and that Coventry was sacrificied to protect Ultra. It is here revealed that a low-grade traffic signal received on 14 November 1940 by a harbour defence command in Antwerp read 'ANGRIFF [attack] KORN', and only later was it discovered that 'Korn' was the code-name for Coventry.

When I read the reminiscences of Carmen Blacker, published in *Codebreakers*, my heart leapt in recognition. She mentions her billet in Wolverton, so similar to mine in discomfort, and her pay of £2 per week – less than mine on grounds that she was younger. Her comment, 'Today I marvel at the trust the Foreign Office placed on people's uncomplaining sense of partiotism in daring to risk such low pay for such highly secret work', is surely one that must be echoed by all who toiled at Bletchley Park.

In 1991 there was held at Bletchley Park a first reunion of the codebreakers and I was surprised and delighted that among those present out of all the thousands who had worked there were four old friends whom I had not seen since 1944.

ENIGMA

In 1992 the Bletchley Park Trust was formed with the specific object of acquiring the site (then owned in an odd co-operative management by the Department of the Environment, British Telecom and the Government Land Agency) and of creating a heritage museum to recognise the vital role played by the Enigma codebreakers in shortening the War. After a long battle against potential developers the Park was acquired in 1999.

The publication in 1995 of Robert Harris's highly acclaimed novel *Enigma* caught the atmosphere of Bletchley brilliantly: all the more remarkable since he is of a later generation and had no first-hand experience of the Park. This book, and the very successful television series *Station X*, have transformed a most secret organisation, of which the public had only limited awareness, into something that is almost a cult, with an eager following of readers and viewers.

The latest Enigma book, by Hugh Sebag-Montefiore, deals largely with the breaking of the German naval Enigma, and highlights the crucial episode of the capture by the Royal Navy of an Enigma machine from a U-boat in 1941. This very episode, which cost the lives of two gallant sailors (drowned with the crippled submarine sank, and both posthumously awarded the George Cross) has itself now been made part of an otherwise fictitious tale forming a new Hollywood epic *U-571* which shows yet again how the United States won the War, even in events and theatres in which its forces were barely or not at all involved. Yes, indeed: Enigma is news.

Equally celebrated are the exploits of the SAS. The regiment's history and ethos are still being capitalised upon. Works on the subject are legion: a stream of books deal with its activities, and there are even 'complete encyclopaedias' featuring tactics, weapons and equipment. Most of these works concentrate on the post-Second World War SAS. The regiment's involvement in many small-scale military campaigns, in counter insurgency and guerrilla operations, on counter-terrorist duties in Northern Ireland and elsewhere, and the participation of units of the SAS in the Gulf War have continued to fascinate the military-minded public. Books – often not approved by the Regiment and the Ministry of Defence – generally portray a 'macho' organisation far removed indeed from the original ideal of Sir David Stirling in the Western Desert and from Leslie Cairns's 'little band of happy warriors' in 1944. The incident of the loss of Leslie and his men has featured in a couple of these SAS books; but the taste has primarily been for narratives of the Andy McNab kind.

My connection with the SAS Regiment and with Leslie's military career continues. In 1991 the SAS celebrated its Golden Jubilee, and I was invited to the Scottish celebrations. These included a Beating Retreat ceremony at Edinburgh Castle where I had the privilege of meeting Viscount Slim, General Sir Peter de la Billière and Sir Fitzroy Maclean. At Dreghorn Barracks we were able to inspect vintage jeeps of the kind that Leslie's team would have used behind the lines, with their rudimentary yet crudely effective twin machine guns. With the help of the Very Revd Dr Fraser McLuskey I made some fresh regimental contacts, and one senior officer of a more recent vintage attempted to shed further light on the mystery of the disappearance of the aircraft taking Leslie and his men to the Morvan. With the passing of time the silence, profound late in the War and after, grows ever more so. What seems increasingly to have been a tragic instance of 'friendly fire' (as we have learned to call it, from more recent conflicts) appears to have been wilfully forgotten, or even hushed up. The absence of information in official records, and the continuing reticence, is hard to understand after more than half a century.

A memorial to all SAS personnel – of French and Belgian SAS units as well as our own Regiment – killed in the campaign for the liberation of France has been erected at Sennecey-le-Grand in the Morvan. This seems to have been a quasi-official French enterprise. Leslie's name is here inscribed, his middle initial spelled incorrectly as 'J'. I was first informed of this by an Edinburgh history graduate who has a house in France. She was reading *Enigma Variations* on holiday in the area, and went to see the site in order, as she said, to pay tribute to a fellow Edinburgh historian. In 1994 I had the satisfaction of seeing Leslie's name added, at long last, to the Edinburgh University war memorial. The work was completed on 11 November in time for the Remembrance Day service that year. Leslie's remaining cousin and I had lobbied for this omission to be rectified, and we were pleased to see it done some fifty years after the event.

On a Nile cruise I used a day free in Cairo to take a taxi to the battlefield of El Alamein where Leslie had fought. War cemeteries are always hauntingly beautiful; but here the gravestones are on sand amid madder-pink oleanders. By extraordinary coincidence the first name I saw, before I had time to look for it, was that of Leslie's cousin Ernest Gardner. In Tunisia some years later I visited the Commonwealth military cemetery at Medjez-el-Bab and came upon several Ayrshire Yeomary graves, including those of two of Leslie's former commanding officers. I saw, too, Wadi Akarit and the remains of the formidable fortifications of the Mareth Line where Leslie had had a hard fight. In Italy I have at various times seen the ground on which the Ayrshire Yeomanry fought in 1943–1945, and where, had the circumstances been different, Leslie might have served and, accordingly, I might not have written this book. At 11 a.m. on the fiftieth anniversary of VE-Day in May 1995 I was at the Stone of Remembrance in that most beautiful and touching of British war cemeteries which lies below the walls of Rome and in the shadow of the Pyramid of Cestius.

In 1994, sponsored by the SAS, I went to Normandy on the British Legion Pilgrimage in commemoration of the fiftieth anniversary of D-Day. My son accompanied me. The Memorial to the Missing at Bayeux is dignified and impressive, but it is on the opposite side of the road from the main cemetery. This seems especially poignant: these are men apart in remembrance as in death. Memories of the day endure: of the Duke of Edinburgh reading from *The Pilgrim's Progress* ('My sword I give to him that shall succeed me in my pilgrimage...'); of my meeting the Prime Minister, John Major; of how we stood in the rain next to some old soldiers of the Warwickshires, and of how they were so pleased that my son knew that this had been Monty's regiment; of how on the beach at Arromanches I had the unusual experience of turning round to see that the tall and distinguished gentleman behind me was wearing the Victoria Cross. I myself had opened the case in which Leslie's medals normally hang in my study, and proudly wore them, as a widow should.

The touching 'Forces Sweethearts' exhibition at the Imperial War Museum, held in 1993, featured my wedding photograph and album pages chronicling our romance. The letters from Leslie which figure so largely in the present book will go eventually to the Department of Documents at the Museum. On a recent visit I noticed that the 25-

pounder gun which forms part of the museum's current display of Second World War weaponry and ordnance was used at Alamein by the 11th Field Regiment, Royal Artillery, with which Leslie fought in the battle. Who knows: perhaps this very gun was one of his troop?

My old Maquisard friend Dr Jean Feigelson (Ika), holder of the Croix de Guerre and the Médaille Militaire, was in 1997 awarded the Légion d'Honneur and I was privileged to be invited to the ceremony in Paris. I had seen Ika a couple of times since this book was first published, and his continuing friendship, founded in a shared wartime experience, is characteristic of what *Enigma Variations* has meant to me over the past ten years. The book has brought me renewed contacts with old friends, and introductions to new ones. I have received more than 130 letters, very many from strangers, and have been deeply touched by this evidence of interest in and empathy with a world and a time that now seem to many like ancient history, but which to me remain as fresh as if it were but yesterday.

I.T.
June 2000